INTERACTIVITIES

• Critical Thinking • Interactive Conversation/Writing • Problem-Solving

InterActivities

James Kohn

• Critical Thinking • Interactive Conversation/Writing • Problem-Solving

HARCOURT BRACE ESL/EFL

Harcourt Brace & Company

Orlando San Diego New York
Toronto London Sydney Tokyo

Permissions Department
Harcourt Brace & Company
6277 Sea Harbor Drive
Orlando, Florida 32887-6777.

Executive Editor:	Frank Crane
Production Manager:	Anne Burkett
Production Assistant:	Deneen Casey
Production & Design:	Mark Kellum, Success by Design, Inc.
Illustrators:	Gary Undercuffler David Herrick
Editorial Concept & Design:	Marilyn Rosenthal, Syntactix International

Printed in the United States of America

ISBN: 0-15-599679-7

4 5 6 7 8 9 0 1 2 3 085 9 8 7 6 5 4 3 2 1

To my wife, Elaine Fischer-Kohn, with love

Acknowledgments

I received much help in preparing this book from two people at Harcourt Brace ESL/EFL: Marilyn Rosenthal, Consulting Director, and Frank Crane, Executive Editor.

I would like to thank Marilyn for encouraging me to start designing the text, and for contributing her judgment toward the format of the book.

I would like especially to thank Frank Crane for his steadfast and productive help in revising and polishing the text and design of the book. He shared with me a clear focus on the strategy of the text, and helped mightily to keep the book "user-friendly."

Without the help of these two people, such a text could never have emerged, and I am very grateful to them.

Contents

Introduction: How To Use InterActivities

Unit Format
Below is a brief guide to the elements of an InterActivities Unit. Teachers may find many other ways to use the activities and assignments in the book; what is included here is only the beginning of ways the book may be used.

Whole-Class Presentations
Each Unit begins with a Whole-Class Presentation, in which students refer to the color illustration on the opening page to introduce themselves to the Unit's topic—for example, talking about distances (Unit 2) or making predictions (Unit 14). The Whole-Class Presentation sets up a context for the topic, and serves as a model for the discovery procedures that follow.

The teacher introduces the topic of the Unit through reference to the Whole-Class Presentation, and may supplement it with additional information to make the theme clear and relevant to her/his students. The teacher may wish to add more examples for illustration and explanation during this part of the Unit. Also, if needed, grammar work may be inserted here.

InterActivities
These form the core of the book. Students form pairs or small groups, and perform group tasks which develop and expand the topic introduced in the Whole-Class Presentation. The InterActivities tasks are practical and grounded in the life experiences of the students. For example, in Unit 3 students work together to measure the size of a home, and plan the living space by placing furniture models in a diagram of each of the rooms. The discussions the InterActivity generates directly reflect real-life plans the students may have regarding rooms in their own homes.

In working through the InterActivities, students employ their knowledge of English to communicate with each other, to solve real-world problems, and to share values. Graphics for the InterActivities, including spot illustrations, charts, and diagrams, help students focus on the tasks. Many InterActivities culminate in short, sentence-level writing assignments. The InterActivities build on each other, preparing students for the longer writing assignment that culminates each lesson.

What You Need to Know/What You Need to Bring:
Some of the InterActivities have inset boxes which contain necessary information.

WHAT YOU NEED TO KNOW boxes provide—in simple, graphic form—the information which students use in completing the tasks assigned.

WHAT YOU NEED TO BRING boxes list everyday materials that the students will use in completing the tasks. Teachers should note these boxes, and prepare the students to bring the needed materials to class, or supply those materials for the students.

If the boxes contain vocabulary words or concepts which are unfamiliar to students, the teacher can use this occasion to introduce the meaning of these new words, or to introduce new language material.

Read, Write and Discuss
In these InterActivities, students practice reading and paraphrasing by reading a passage for understanding, then rewriting their own version of the passage from memory. When they have finished writing, they compare their versions with other students' versions, and gain insight about how to retain and to express the meaning of what they have read.

Writing Assignments

The final InterActivity in each Unit is a writing assignment, in which students follow a process of discussion, discovery of a topic, writing a draft, revision through peer-editing, proofreading for errors, and rewriting a final draft. By completing these tasks, students learn a process which they may employ in future writing assignments, whether in daily life or in an academic setting. The teacher may use these writing assignments as an evaluative tool to check on students' progress. Students should keep their writing in a folder, as part of their portfolio of writing.

Review Units

Unit Eight and Unit Fifteen recap skills that the students have learned in previous Units, and may be used as evaluative Units. For example, the teacher may wish to use the InterActivities in these Units to test how well the students have learned to interact with other students. The writing assignments in these Units may be done in class, as a testing instrument or diagnostic tool, to find out whether particular students need additional help.

Grammar and Reading

Reading skills are practiced in each Unit in the text, through the use of charts, graphs, short paragraphs, and longer passages. Reading is integrated into the holistic understanding that students bring to the activities in the Units. In addition, there are specific reading assignments, as outlined in the Read, Write and Discuss activities described above. Although this text includes no specifically-designed grammar exercises, students are asked to proofread all of their writing assignments for grammar problems. Teachers may wish to complement the book with grammar exercises, if needed.

"To the Teacher"

At the end of some Units, there are notes to the teacher, intended to help teachers supplement the lessons, or to supply extra information. Teachers may want to read these notes for suggestions to amplify their teaching.

A Final Word

InterActivities is designed to be self-sufficient, and to provide students with an initiation to writing. The book also fits into multiple-skills classes, in which the teacher also presents grammar, reading, speaking, and other English-language skills. The spirit of the book is one of discovery. The writer hopes teachers will make their own discoveries while helping students make theirs.

Unit 1

WHERE AM I?

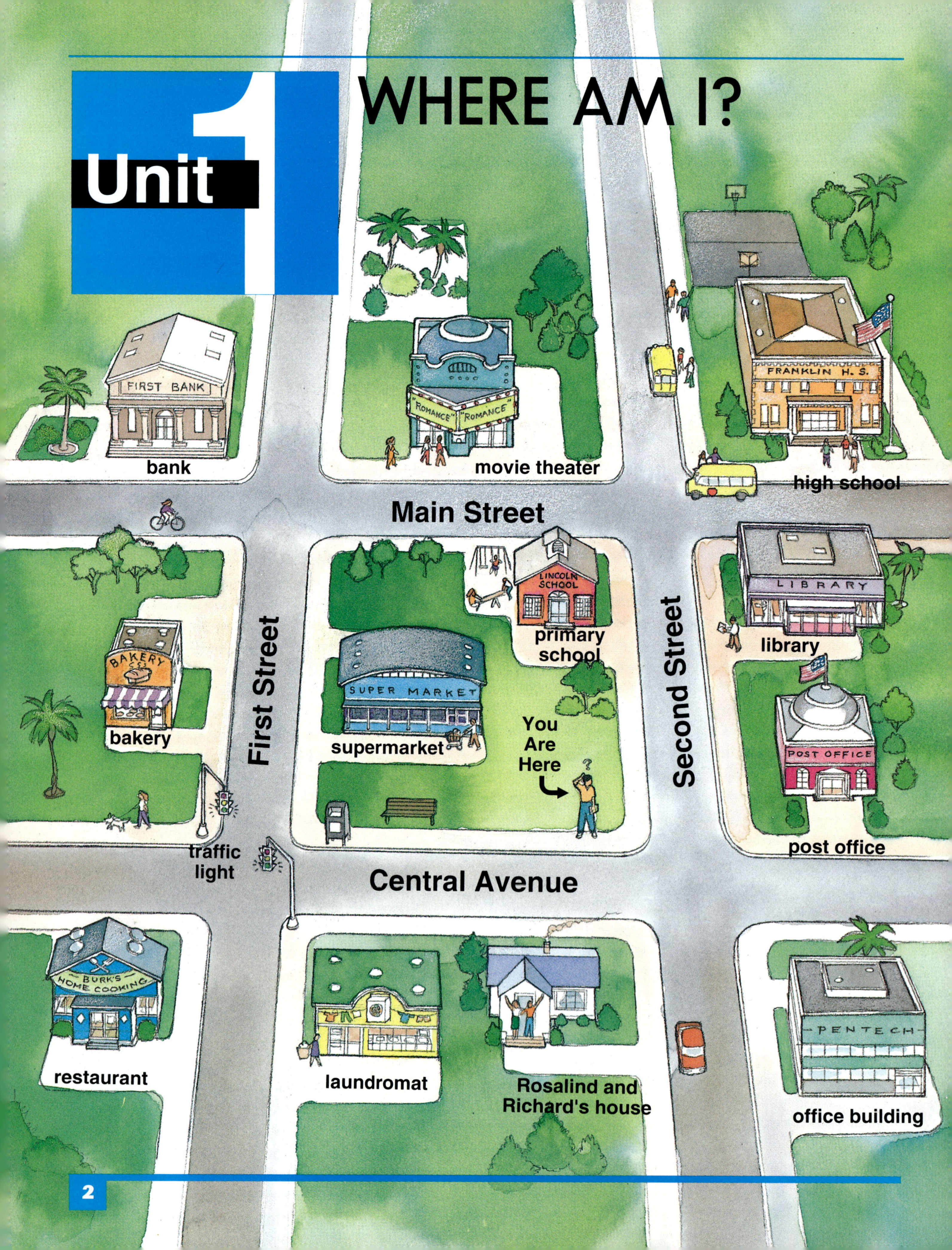

WHOLE CLASS

PRESENTATION LET'S TALK ABOUT LOCATIONS

It is difficult to find your way around a city when you have just arrived. In this Unit, you will find out how to describe locations, how to ask for directions to find addresses, and how to give directions to people. By the end of the Unit, you will be an expert at telling people where you are.

To tell people where to find a certain location, we often use some of the following expressions:

On the corner of X Street and Y Avenue means that the location is at the place where X Street crosses Y Avenue.

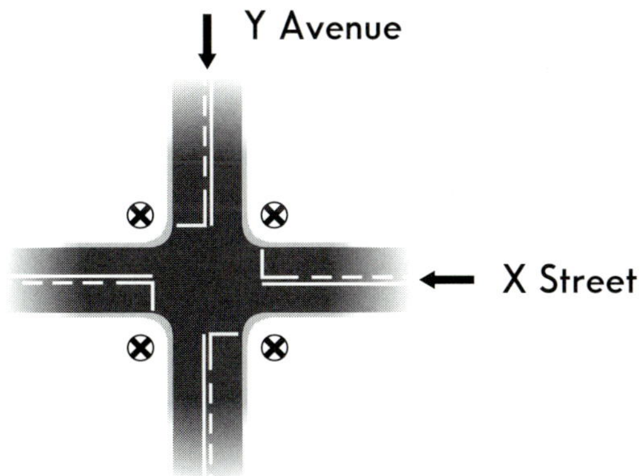

Around the corner from X Building means that the location is on the street that crosses the street near X Building.

Three blocks from here means that the location is three crossing streets from where we are now located.

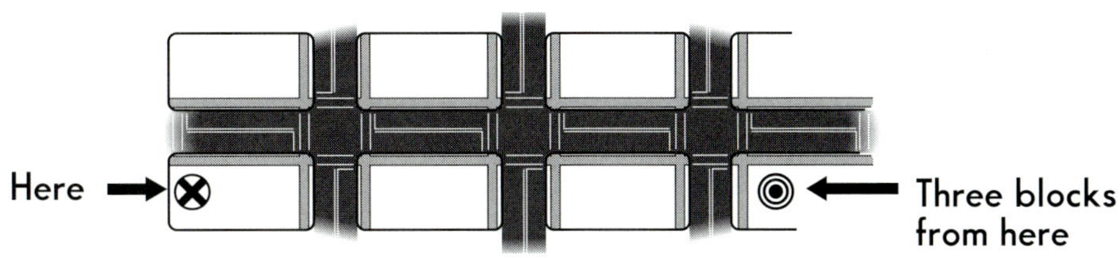

Across the street from here means that the location is on the other side of the street.

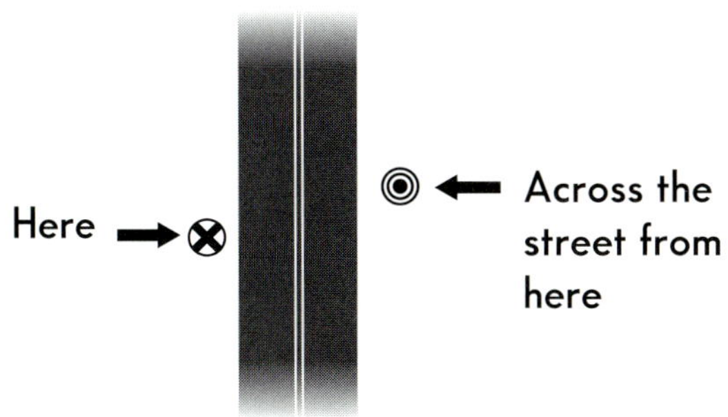

On the left means on the left-hand side of a street. **On the right** means on the right-hand side of a street.

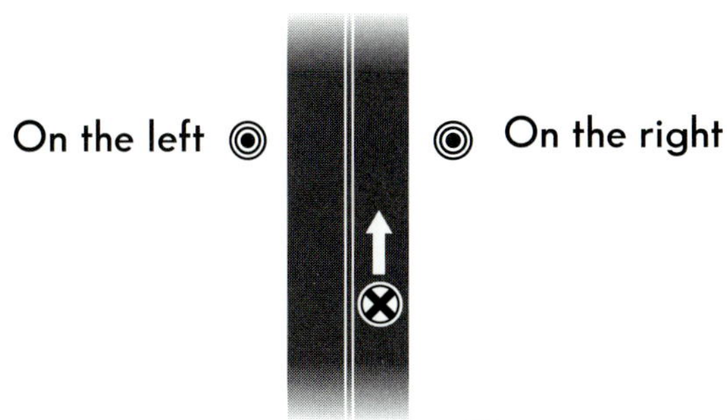

(See next page.)

(Whole-Class Presentation, Continued.)

1. Look at the map on page 2. Then fill in the blank with the correct expression.

on the corner of	on the right	one block from
across the street from	around the corner	

a. The bakery is ______________________________ the supermarket.

b. As you walk along First Street from Central Avenue to Main Street, you see that the supermarket is ______________________________.

c. The high school is ______________________________ the Pentech office building.

d. From Rosalind and Richard's house, walk toward First Street. You see that the laundromat is ______________________________.

e. The restaurant is ______________________________ First Street and Central Avenue.

2. Describe the location of the following places on the map on page 2.

a. The bank ______________________________

b. The post office ______________________________

c. The high school ______________________________

d. The supermarket ______________________________

e. The primary school ______________________________

INTER ACTIVITY 1 USING A MAP

Look at the map on page 2. With a partner, find each of the following locations, and draw lines from the spot marked YOU ARE HERE to each location.

a. the bakery
b. the movie theater
c. the laundromat
d. the supermarket
e. the post office
f. the high school

Now practice asking about locations with your partner. For example, one person will ask, "How do you get to the laundromat from here?" *and the partner will answer,* "Go to the corner of Central and First, and turn left." *Take turns with your partner asking for directions, and answering. After a while, your teacher will ask YOU for directions, so you will have to know how to answer.*

INTER ACTIVITY 2 GIVING DIRECTIONS

Your teacher will divide the class into groups of four people. In your group, study the map and decide how to answer the questions below. Use the following steps.

a. Read your answers aloud.

b. Write down the correct answer in the space below the question.

c. When you have answered all the questions, check your sentences with the others in your group.

d. Remember: Start all directions from Richard and Rosalind's house.

Answer the following questions.

1. From Richard and Rosalind's house, where is the supermarket?

____

2. Where is the primary school?

____

3. Where is the movie theater?

____

4. Where is the bakery?

____

5. Where is the laundromat?

____

6. Where is the post office?

____

7. Where is the high school?

____

8. Where is the savings bank?

____

9. Where is the traffic light?

____

10. Where is the mailbox?

____

INTERACTIVITY 3 FINDING YOUR WAY AROUND THE NEIGHBORHOOD

With your group, draw a map of the neighborhood around the school where you are now studying. (Use the space below or a separate piece of paper.) Be sure to include the names of the streets and the locations of some of the stores, shops, and services in the area. You may decide to include the bus stops closest to the school in your map.

Talk about your map as follows:

a. Cover the map with a piece of paper.

b. Each group member in turn asks a question about how to get from the school to a place on the map.

c. Each other group member, in turn, tries to answer the question.

d. The group checks to see whether the answer is correct.

e. If the answer is correct, the questioner asks another question. If the answer is wrong, a new student gets to ask the questions.

INTER ACTIVITY 4 WRITING A LETTER

WHAT YOU NEED TO KNOW:

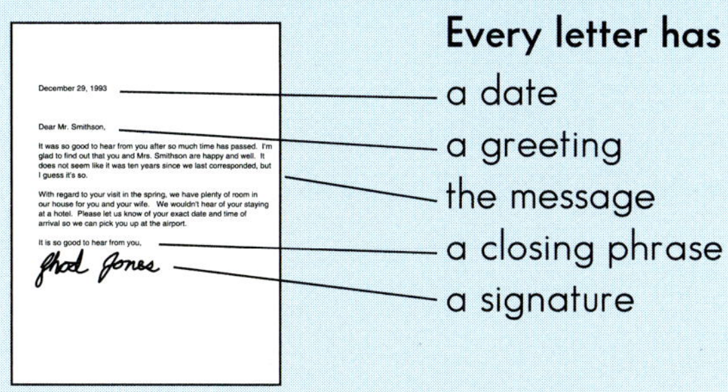

1. In the space below, write a letter to your classmates about your neighborhood. Be sure to tell the location of the nearest

a. supermarket

b. bank

c. post office

d. coffee shop or restaurant

e. public school

Date: ___________

Dear __________________,

I'd like to tell you about where I live. ________________________________

____

____

____

____

Sincerely yours,

____

2. Read a classmate's letter and write one or two sentences in answer to it.

____

____

INTER ACTIVITY 5 HELPING TOURISTS AROUND YOUR CITY

1. With a small group of students, imagine that you are helping tourists in your city to find their way to some of the main attractions. Use the following steps:

a. Decide on five places which you think tourists should visit. You should choose places which everyone wants to see. You may want to choose some special places that most people don't visit.

b. Choose a central location where the tourists start the tour. This place may be a famous tourist hotel or a large public square in the center of the city.

c. Plan a route for the visit. Decide which spot they should visit first, then second, third, fourth, and last. Decide whether the tourists can use buses, taxis, or cars. Remember to allow time to eat lunch!

d. Write an outline of the tour. In the spaces below, write the list of places the tourists will visit, including the transportation from one place to the next, and the place for lunch.

TOUR OUTLINE

First stop: ______________________ How to get there: ____________________

____

Second stop: ____________________ How to get there: ____________________

____

Third stop: ______________________ How to get there: ____________________

____

Lunch: ______________________________________

Fourth stop: _____________________ How to get there: ____________________

____

Fifth stop: ______________________ How to get there: ____________________

____

2. Compare your list with other groups' lists. If you came to your city as a tourist, which tour would you like to take?

INTERACTIVITY 6 WRITING A TOURIST BROCHURE

WHAT YOU NEED TO BRING:

a list of places to visit

photographs

colored paper

a pair of scissors

glue

With a group, use one of the lists of tourist areas which you completed in InterActivity 5. Design a tourist brochure to attract people to the tour. Be sure to use the following elements in your brochure:

a. **A headline.** One short phrase tells about your tour—for example, "Short Tour for Busy People."

b. **A list of places to visit.** Each place should have one sentence describing its interesting features.

c. **A short description of your tour lunch.** Tourists expect to have lunch in a nice place with a good view.

d. **Special features.** Since there are other tours which people can choose, you need to describe something very special about your tour, different from all the others.

e. **Pictures.** Use photographs or drawings in your brochure to add liveliness and make your brochure very attractive. If possible, use different colors in the final copy.

1. *Begin by making a draft version of the brochure, with all the features listed above.*
2. *Make changes to make the brochure easy to read and attractive.*
3. *When you have made the changes, put the brochure together using colored paper and pictures.*
4. *Show your completed brochure to the other students in the class.*

INTERACTIVITY 7 READ, WRITE, AND DISCUSS

Read the following paragraph to yourself as many times as you can in five minutes. After you have finished reading, cover the paragraph, and then write down what you can remember of the paragraph. Don't worry if you can't remember every word. Be sure to use only complete sentences.

Danny has the worst commute I ever heard of. He gets up at 5:00 a.m. every morning, gets dressed, and has a quick breakfast. He catches the number 47 bus, which stops three blocks from his house, on Broadway. He takes the bus to the train station, where he takes the 5:45 a.m. train into the city. Then he walks around the corner and down the street five blocks to school. He gets to school at 7:45. If he is lucky, he has just enough time for a snack before class begins.

1. Write about Danny's commute in your own words:

____

____

____

____

____

2. Write about a friend who has a commute like Danny's:

____

____

____

____

____

INTERACTIVITY 8 WRITING ABOUT COMMUTES

Getting to work or to school is a big problem for many people. It takes most North Americans about half an hour or more to get to where they are going in the morning, and to return home at night. But some people have an easier time than others. In this InterActivity, you are going to find out about the commutes of the other people in your class, and write a report about these commutes.

1. Interview classmates. You and a partner each interview at least four different people in your class. Ask the following questions on the chart below:

QUESTIONS	1st PERSON	2nd PERSON	3rd PERSON	4th PERSON
a. What is your name, please?	________	________	________	________
b. How far away from the school do you live?	________	________	________	________
c. How do you come to school?	________	________	________	________
d. Which bus or train do you take?	________	________	________	________
e. If you work, which bus or train do you take from work to school?	________	________	________	________
f. How long does it usually take to come to school?	________	________	________	________

2. Compare notes. With your partner, compare notes from the interviews. Decide which person whom you interviewed has the longest commute to school, and to work. Tell your partner whether that person has to take the bus or train, and when he or she must leave home to arrive in time.

3. Write a report. On a separate piece of paper, write a report about the longest commute which you found. Your report might start like this:

"We interviewed several people to find out which one had the longest commute to school."

End your report like this:

"But the longest commute was ______________________."

4. Check your report with your partner. Ask him or her to read the report carefully. Check for mistakes. If your partner finds any mistakes, then make changes in your report.

5. Hand in your report. When you have finished, give your report to your teacher.

To the Teacher: You might want to share individual reports with the class.

Unit 2 HOW FAR IS IT?

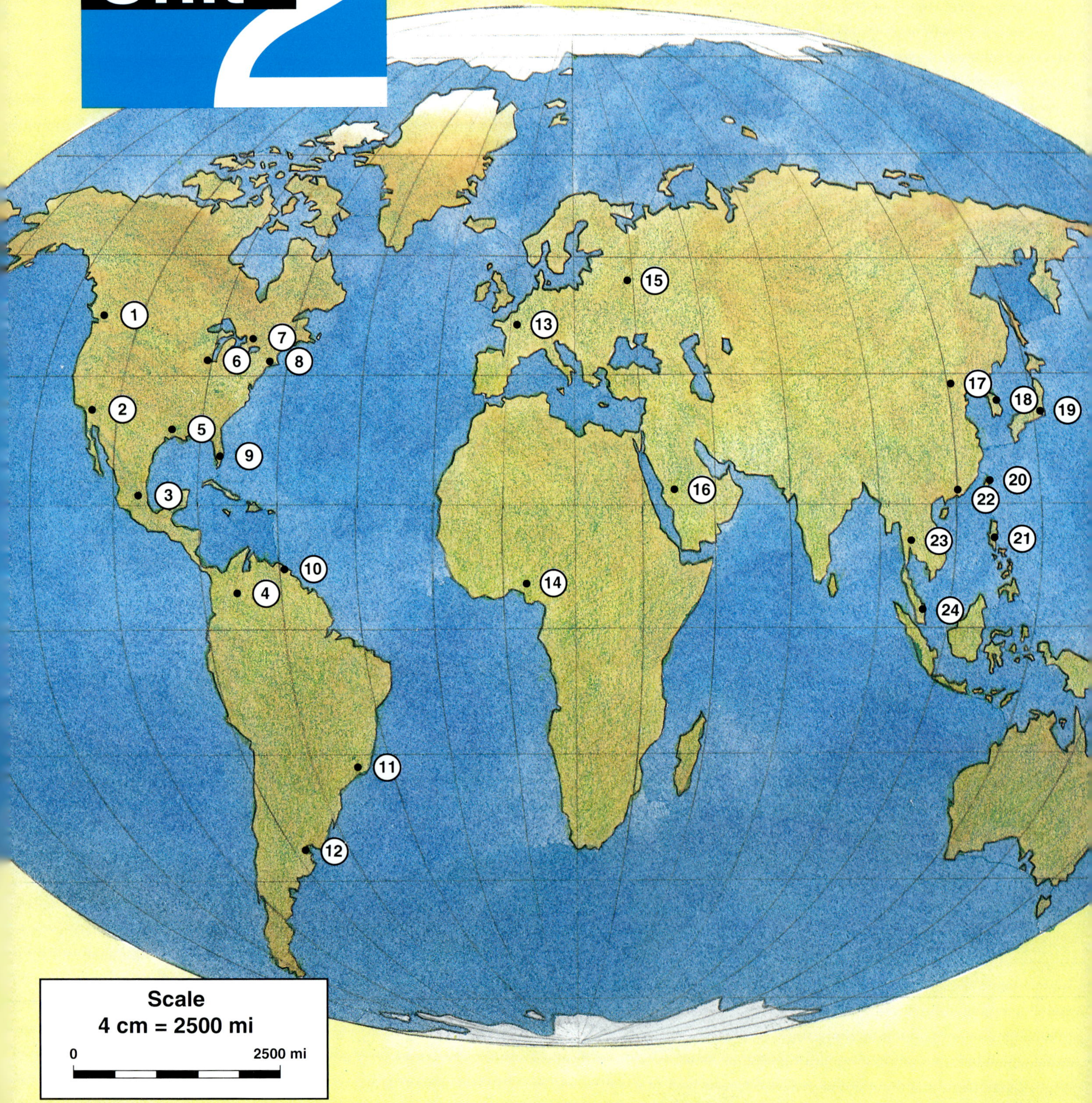

WHOLE CLASS

PRESENTATION FINDING PLACES ON A MAP

Most of us have traveled very far from our homes at some point in our lives. Whenever we travel, we think about how far we have to go, how long it will take to arrive, and how we can decide on whether to take the bus, the train, or go by car. In this Unit, we are going to learn how to talk about distances, travel, and travel times.

Look at the map of the world on page 12. Listed below are some famous cities you can find on the map. Perhaps you can find some of the places where you have been or where you would like to travel. Your teacher will help you locate some of these places, if you need help.

1. Look at the list of cities below. Next to the name of each city, write the number of its location from the map on page 12.

a. Bangkok ________	i. Kuala Lumpur ___	q. New York _______
b. Beijing __________	j. Lagos __________	r. Paris ___________
c. Bogotá __________	k. Los Angeles _____	s. Rio de Janeiro ___
d. Buenos Aires ____	l. Manila __________	t. Seoul ___________
e. Caracas ________	m. Mecca __________	u. Taipei ___________
f. Chicago ________	n. Mexico City ______	v. Tokyo ___________
g. Hong Kong ______	o. Miami ___________	w. Toronto _________
h. Houston _________	p. Moscow _________	x. Vancouver ______

When you are ready to check your answers, turn your book upside down and see the Answer Key on this page.

2. On the map, find the North American cities which are farthest away from you. Write their names below:

____

3. Now write the names of the world cities on the map which are farthest away from you:

____

Answer Key: a.23 b.17 c.4 d.12 e.10 f.6 g.22 h.5 i.24 j.14 k.2 l.21 m.16 n.3 o.9 p.15 q.8 r.13 s.11 t.18 u.20 v.19 w.7 x.1

INTER ACTIVITY 1 MEASURING DISTANCES

WHAT YOU NEED TO BRING:

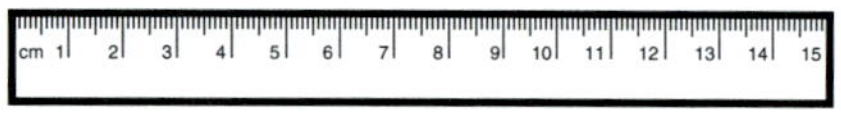
a ruler marked in centimeters

a pencil with an eraser

a calculator

WHAT YOU NEED TO KNOW:

scale = an exact way to compare the size of a map or plan with the original. On the map on page 12, 4 centimeters (cm) represents 2,500 miles.

1. Form a group of three people to work on the distances between cities, like this:

a. Choose five cities from the list in the Whole Class Presentation.

b. Using the map on page 12, draw a line from where you are now to the first city.

c. Measure the distance in centimeters.

d. Convert the centimeter measurement to miles.

e. Write the distance in the chart below.

f. Continue the same procedure with the other four cities.

2. Write the cities and distances in the chart below.

STARTING FROM	DESTINATION CITY	HOW FAR AWAY?
New York	Buenos Aires	6,000 miles
____________	____________	____________
____________	____________	____________
____________	____________	____________
____________	____________	____________
____________	____________	____________

3. *When you have finished measuring the distances, report what you have found by writing out a sentence for each location—for example,*

"Buenos Aires is about 6,000 miles from New York."

INTERACTIVITY 2 WRITING ABOUT DISTANCES

WHAT YOU NEED TO BRING:

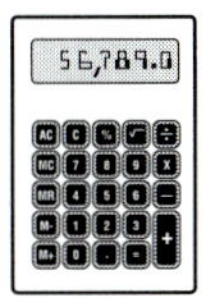

a calculator

WHAT YOU NEED TO KNOW:

Most countries in the world use the metric system of millimeters, centimeters, meters, and kilometers. In the U.S., short distances are measured by inch, foot, and yard. Longer distances are measured by mile, 1/2 mile, or 1/4 mile.

1 foot (ft) = 30.5 cm
1 yard (yd) = 3 ft = 0.92 m
1 mile = 1.6 km

1 cm = 0.4 inches (in.)
1 m = 39.37 in. = 3.28 ft
1 km = 0.62 mi

Now figure out the distance in kilometers for the cities you have measured in the last activity. For instance, the distance from New York to Buenos Aires is about 10,000 kilometers.

On a separate piece of paper, write sentences in which you convert the distances in miles which you found in InterActivity 1. For example, you might write

"The distance from New York to Buenos Aires is about 10,000 kilometers."

INTER ACTIVITY 3 MEASURING SMALL DISTANCES

In this InterActivity, you are going to figure out small distances in both inches and centimeters. You will need to use both inch and centimeter measures.

WHAT YOU NEED TO BRING:

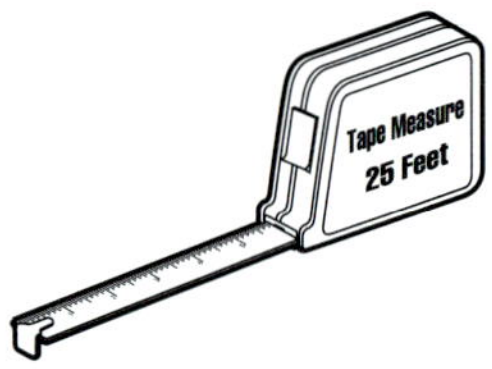

a tape measure or a ruler marked in inches or centimeters

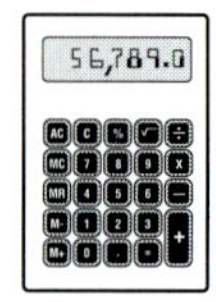

a calculator

WHAT YOU NEED TO KNOW:

Three feet = 1 yard (3 ft = 1 yd)
One m = 3.28 ft
One inch (1 in.) = 2.5 centimeters (2.5 cm)
One cm = 0.4 in.

Answer the following questions. Use feet and inches as well as meters and centimeters.

1. What are the dimensions (height and width) of this page?

Answer: _______in high by ______in wide. Or _______cm high by ______cm wide.

2. How tall is each person in the group in feet/inches and meters/centimeters? (Continue on a separate piece of paper, if necessary.)

NAME:	HEIGHT: FEET/INCHES	HEIGHT: METERS/CENTIMETERS
____________________	____________________	____________________
____________________	____________________	____________________
____________________	____________________	____________________
____________________	____________________	____________________
____________________	____________________	____________________

3. How far is it from your desk to the nearest wall?

Answer:__________ ft, _____________ in. Or ______________ m, ___________ cm

4. How long is your shoe?

Answer:________ in. Or ________ cm

5. How long is your desk or table?

Answer:________ in. Or ________ cm

INTER ACTIVITY 4 FIGURING OUT COMMUTING TIMES

1. With a partner, study the following chart of distances and commute times from a major city called "Metropolis" to the smaller cities around it:

CITY	DISTANCE FROM METROPOLIS	COMMUTE TIME (BY CAR)
Albany	20 miles	45 minutes
Bridgetown	10 miles	40 minutes
Concord	40 miles	55 minutes
Dover	30 miles	45 minutes
Eastridge	15 miles	30 minutes

2. Which city is furthest from Metropolis? Put a check (√) by your choices for a-d.

a. Albany ________or Concord? ________

b. Eastridge ______ or Bridgetown? _____

c. Dover _________or Albany? _________

d. Dover _________ or Concord? _______

3. With your partner, write sentences comparing the following pairs of cities on the chart by distances from Metropolis. For example, you might write

"Albany is ten miles farther from Metropolis than Bridgetown."

a. Albany and Dover: ____

____

b. Concord and Albany: ____

____

c. Bridgetown and Eastridge: ____

____

d. Concord and Eastridge: ____

____

e. Dover and Bridgetown: ____

____

(See next page.)

(InterActivity 4, continued.)

4. Now with your partner, write sentences comparing the following pairs of cities on the chart by commute times from Metropolis. For example, you might write

"It takes five minutes longer to commute to Metropolis from Albany than from Bridgetown."

a. Albany and Dover: ______________________________

____

b. Concord and Albany: ______________________________

____

c. Bridgetown and Eastridge: ______________________________

____

d. Concord and Eastridge: ______________________________

____

e. Dover and Bridgetown: ______________________________

____

5. With your partner, write sentences comparing both distance and time for cities on the chart. For example,

"It takes five more minutes to commute to Metropolis from Albany than it does from Bridgetown. Also the trip is ten miles longer."

____

____

____

____

____

____

____

____

INTER ACTIVITY 5 READ, WRITE, AND DISCUSS

Read the following paragraph as many times as you can in five minutes. After you have finished reading, cover the paragraph and then write down what you can remember of the paragraph. Don't worry if you can't remember every word.

I like living here in Eastridge, but my friends think I am crazy. I know it takes thirty minutes to commute into the city. I know there are very few people on the streets after 5 p.m. I know there is only one fresh grocery store in the town. But I still like it more than I like the city. Here there is more space than in the city. The air is cleaner here, and there is less noise than in the city. When I go to the shopping mall, I can see many people, and I can shop in more stores in one visit than I can in the city.

1. *Write the meaning in your own words:*

____

____

____

____

____

____

____

____

____

____

____

____

2. *With your group, discuss the meaning of the paragraph.*

INTER ACTIVITY 6 WORD PROBLEMS

1. With two other students, form a small group to solve the following problems:

a. Maria has three ways to come to school—by bus, by car, or on foot. If she walks, it takes her forty minutes, and it's free of charge, but she sometimes feels cold, tired, or frightened. If she rides the bus, it costs $1.00, but it might take an hour, because the bus is often late. If she takes her car, it takes only ten minutes, but she must spend $5.00 in parking charges and gasoline, or risk getting a ticket on the street. Maria does not have much money to spend on transportation. Which transportation choice should she make, and why?

Choice: ____________________

Reasons: ____________________

____

____

b. Kim wants to visit his friend in the state capital for the weekend. The city is two hours by car from his home, or three hours by train, or four hours by bus. Buses run more frequently than trains, and are less expensive. Trains are faster and more elegant than buses, but they are less convenient. Cars are more convenient than either buses or trains, but Kim does not own a car, so he must rent one, or borrow one from a friend. Imagine that you are Kim's friend. What do you advise him to do?

Choice: ____________________

Reasons: ____________________

____

____

2. Compare your answers with those of other groups.

3. Do you know of someone with a problem like Maria's or Kim's? Write about the problem here:

____

____

____

INTER ACTIVITY 7 WRITING ABOUT COMMUTE TIMES

WHAT YOU NEED TO BRING:

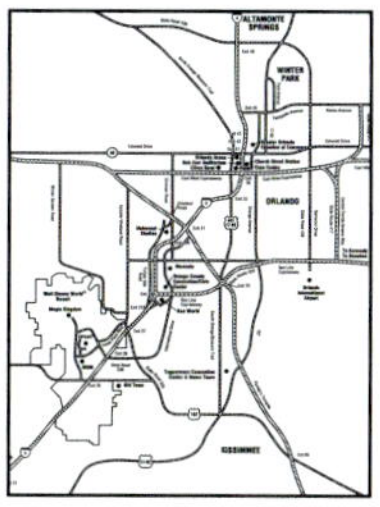

a map of your local area

With your group, find the distance from the nearest large city to three of the surrounding suburbs. Make a guess about how long it takes to drive one way from the suburb to the city. When you have the information, write it on the chart below.

SUBURB	DISTANCE FROM THE CITY	COMMUTE TIME (BY CAR)
______________	__________ miles	______________ minutes
______________	__________ miles	______________ minutes
______________	__________ miles	______________ minutes

1. Discuss the following questions with your group:

a. Which suburb has a longer commute to the city than the others?

b. Which suburb has a shorter commute time?

c. Which suburb has a more comfortable commute?

d. Which suburb has the best bus or train service?

2. After you have considered these questions, write a one-paragraph report about what you have found:

____

____

____

____

____

Unit 3 HOW BIG IS IT?

PRESENTATION MEASURING A "BLUEPRINT"

WHOLE CLASS

It's often very important to know the size of various things—rooms, pieces of furniture, packages. In this Unit, we will study how to talk about the measurement of the size of these items. To help us, we need to use a measuring instrument. Make sure that you have a ruler or a tape measure to use as you work through this lesson. Refer back to Unit 2 for help with U.S. and metric measurements.

WHAT YOU NEED TO BRING:

a ruler or a tape measure marked in inches

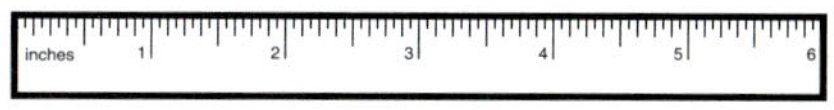

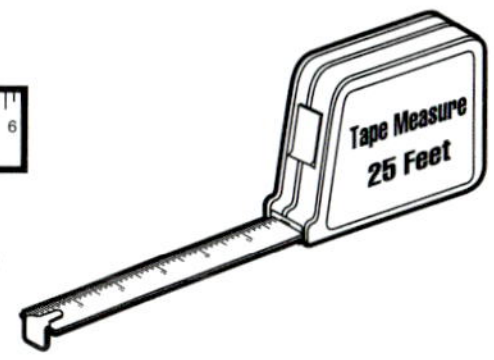

The picture on page 22 is a diagram of a two-bedroom apartment. When such diagrams are printed on blue paper, they are often called "blueprints." These blueprints can help a contractor plan how to build a house or apartment building. Blueprints can also help us decide which furniture to put in our rooms.

In this drawing, the scale of the dimensions is 1/4 inch to one foot. For example, if one wall in the drawing is 2.5 inches long, it represents 2.5 in. x 4 ft/in. = 10 feet. The actual wall is 10 ft long.

Using a ruler or tape measure, find the length and width in feet of each room in the blueprint. Write them in the chart below.

ROOM	LENGTH	WIDTH
Small Bedroom	______ ft	______ ft
Large Bedroom	______ ft	______ ft
Kitchen	______ ft	______ ft
Bathroom	______ ft	______ ft
Dining Room	______ ft	______ ft
Living Room	______ ft	______ ft

INTERACTIVITY 1 ARRANGING FURNITURE

WHAT YOU NEED TO BRING:

a pencil with an eraser

a pair of scissors

tracing paper

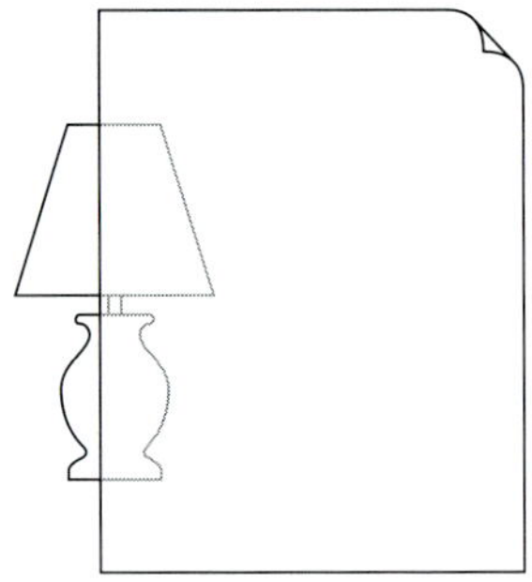

With a small group, make up a list of the furniture you will need to put in the apartment on page 22 so that a family of four people could live there. Here is a partial list:

FURNITURE FOR A FAMILY OF FOUR

beds	lamps
bookcases	refrigerator
chairs	small coffee table
tables	stereo system
crib	stove
desk	stuffed chairs
dining table	television
dressers	work table

1. On a separate piece of paper, add furniture to the list.

2. Using the tracing paper, make furniture cutouts. Trace the pieces of furniture from the picture on page 22 and cut them out with a scissors. (Make other cutouts if necessary, but remember the scale: 1/4 in = 1ft.)

3. Try to fit all the furniture cutouts into the blueprint on page 22. If there is no room for some of the furniture, choose only the most important pieces to include.

4. Talk about the different arrangements of furniture on your blueprint with the other people in your group. Use these steps:

a. Are there problems with any of the arrangements?

b. Which pieces of furniture have you left out? Why?

5. Together, decide which arrangement is your favorite.

INTERACTIVITY 2 YOUR IDEAL APARTMENT

WHAT YOU NEED TO BRING:

blank paper for drawing

a pencil with an eraser

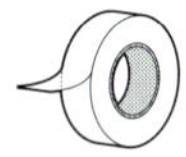
tape or glue for paper

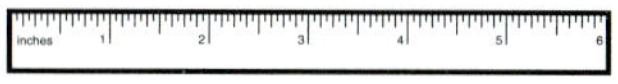
a ruler marked in inches

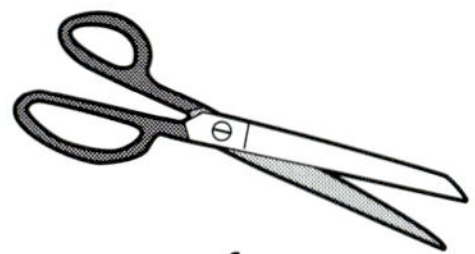
a pair of scissors

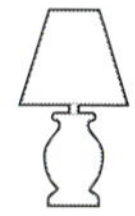
the furniture cutouts from InterActivity 1

With a person from your group, arrange rooms and furniture to make your ideal apartment. Use the following steps:

1. On different pieces of paper, draw rectangles for the rooms in the list below. Use a scale of 1/4 inch = 1 foot. Label each rectangle with the name of a room ("dining room," "living room," etc.). Remember to include doors and windows.

ROOMS

small bedroom (10 ft x 13 ft)	living room (11 ft x 18 ft)
dining room (11 ft x 8 ft)	bathroom (5 ft x 8 ft)
large bedroom (11 ft x 14 ft)	kitchen (8 ft x 11 ft)

2. Arrange the rooms in a way that looks best to both of you. Show your arrangement to your group. Ask for suggestions—for example:

   "How do you like our arrangement?"
   "Maybe the kitchen should be closer to the front door."

3. Look at the list of furniture below.

sofa (3 ft x 7 ft)	armchair (3 ft x 4 ft)	large table (4 ft x 6 ft)
small table (3 ft x 4 ft)	standing lamp (2 ft x 2 ft)	carpet (6 ft x 9 ft)

Using your furniture cutouts, arrange the furniture as you wish in all the rooms you have drawn. Make sure there is enough space for all the pieces.

4. Ask your group for comments about where you have put the furniture. When you are sure you have the best arrangement, attach the furniture cutouts to the rooms with tape or glue.

5. When you have finished, compare your plans for an ideal apartment with those of the other group members.

INTER ACTIVITY 3 HOME MEASUREMENTS

WHAT YOU NEED TO KNOW:

Some phrases for room locations:

"**on the near wall**" = the wall closest to you
"**on the far wall**" = the wall farthest from you
"**in the middle of the room**" = not close to any wall
"**across the room**" = on the other side of the room

1. Measure a room in your home.

Measure the length of one room in your home, from one wall to the opposite wall. Then measure the length between the other two walls. These two distances give you the dimensions of that room.

If you do not have a ruler or tape measure at home, use your shoes! An average men's shoe is about 1 ft in length; an average women's shoe is about 10 inches in length. Write down the dimensions of the room on a piece of paper.

2. Measure the furniture.

Make a list of all the pieces of furniture in the room. Now measure the length and width of each piece, and write it down on a separate piece of paper.

3. Write a report.

In a short report, describe the length and width of the room, the length and width of the furniture, and where the furniture is located. Begin your report like this:

I measured a room and the furniture in it. Here is what I found.

The room is ________________ wide and ________________ long. ____________________

____

____

____

____

____

____

4. Exchange your report with a partner, and read your partner's report.

5. Draw your partner's room according to the description in his or her report.

6. Show your drawing to your partner. Find out how it compares to the actual room.

INTER ACTIVITY 4 "HOW BIG IS IT?"

WHAT YOU NEED TO BRING:

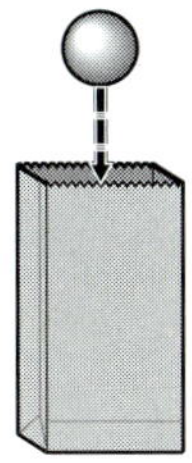

one small object in a paper bag

WHAT YOU NEED TO KNOW:

Words to describe size:

for larger size:	bigger, wider, thicker
for smaller size:	smaller, narrower, thinner
for weight:	lighter, heavier
for shape:	round, square, rectangular, triangular, long, thin, bulky, pointy, flat

For this InterActivity, bring some object to class which you must keep in a paper bag and not show to anyone. You may decide to bring a book, a bottle, a balloon, a loaf of bread, or any other small object. The teacher will divide the class into groups of eight people. Use the following steps:

a. One person begins by saying to the other people in the group, "I've got something in this bag. What is it?"

b. Each person in turn is allowed to ask ONE question only, to estimate the size. He or she might ask, "Is it bigger than a book, or smaller?" The first person answers in a complete sentence: "It's larger than a book." Only questions about size, weight and shape are allowed.

c. It is OK to ask questions like "Is it bigger than my friend's object?"

d. If the questioner thinks of the answer, he or she may ask directly, "Is it a ________?" Each questioner is allowed only one question in each turn. Then the next person in the group gets a turn.

e. When someone has identified the object in the bag, someone else in the group begins the game again, using his or her own object.

INTER ACTIVITY 5 THE RETURN COUNTER

WHAT YOU NEED TO BRING:

an article of clothing that does not fit you—or example, a sweater, a jacket, a pair of shoes, a hat, or anything else which is not your size

In this InterActivity, you are going to pretend to return clothing to the store where you bought it. You are returning it because it is the wrong size. You need to explain that the item is too big, too small, too narrow, and so on. You need to ask for another one that is the correct size.

1. Form small groups for a role-play with these roles:

a. Customers want to return clothing items.

b. Counter persons listen to the customers and respond.

c. Supervisors decide what to do if there is an argument.

Take some time to discuss with your group what the customer will say, what the counter person will answer, and what the supervisor will do. Take turns with the different roles until your group feels comfortable.

2. For each group, choose one customer, one counter person, and one supervisor to act out a scene as follows:

a. The counter person will have to decide if you are right to bring the item back.

b. If the counter person says yes, you will get an exchange.

c. If the counter person says no, then the dialog may continue as you wish.

3. After about fifteen minutes, the teacher will ask you to demonstrate your scene to the other students.

INTER ACTIVITY 6 A MULTIPLE-CHOICE LETTER

In this InterActivity, your group will write a letter to another group, using words which you have chosen. You can have some fun with your choices!

1. Choose a word or phrase from each list below (or think of your own). Write it in the space under the list.

a. **Favorite fruits:** pears, peaches, cherries, apples

Your choice: ______________________________

b. **A word meaning poor quality:** rotten, lousy, awful, sickening

Your choice: ______________________________

c. **What you did when you were angry:** screamed, had a fit, kicked the chair

Your choice: ______________________________

d. **What the Complaint Department always says:**
"We don't have them in stock anymore."
"They aren't so bad."
"I'll have to speak to the supervisor."

Your choice: ______________________________

e. **Favorite junk food:** potato chips, candy, doughnuts, french fries

Your choice: ______________________________

2. Now read the following letter of complaint, which has several blanks. Fill in blanks (a)-(e) with the choices you made in step 1 above. Finally, choose a name for the sender of the letter.

Dear friends,

Something has been bothering me, and I have to write to you about it. I know how much we all like (a) ________________. Well, last week I went shopping to buy you some. But when I got them home, I saw they were (b) ________________. In fact, they were so bad that I (c) ______________________________. I tried to take them back to the store, but they said (d) ______________________________. I told them I bought them for my friends, but they didn't care. They told me I should have bought (e) ________________ instead.

What should I do now? Would you rather have some lousy (a) ________________ or some old (e) ________________?

Your friend,

____

3. Now copy the letter and send it to another group in your class!

INTER ACTIVITY 7 WRITING A LETTER OF COMPLAINT

In this InterActivity, you will write a letter to a store to complain about something you bought which does not work or does not fit. Such letters are sometimes very useful in settling a dispute, as they give you the opportunity to express yourself clearly. If you follow the process outlined below, you may find it is easy to write such letters.

1. *Brainstorm: First gather together your thoughts about your complaint. What did you buy? What happened after you bought it and took it home? Was something wrong with the item before you used it? Did you try to fix it? Did you take it back to the store? What did they tell you when you tried to return it? What do you think the store should do—give your money back, or give you a different item?*

2. *Study the sample letter: Look at the sample letter on page 31, and answer these questions:*

a. Where is the date?

b. How does the letter begin?

c. Where is the address of the store?

d. Where is J. Rivers' address?

e. Where does the word "Sincerely" appear?

3. *Draft a letter: After you have studied the sample letter, write a draft of a letter about your complaint. Remember: Give details about the item, the date you bought it, and the problem with it. Also, be specific about what you want the store to do.*

4. *Pair-edit: Exchange drafts with a partner. As you read your partner's draft, ask yourself:*

a. What did this person buy?

b. When did the person buy the item?

c. What was wrong with the item?

d. What does the person want the store to do?

If you can't answer these questions, tell your partner, so she or he can make changes.

5. *Rewrite:* ***When you get your letter back, write it over again, and make any changes that you think will improve the letter. Look carefully for small grammar and spelling mistakes; if you are not sure about any of the words, ask your teacher.***

6. *Proofread:* ***Exchange papers with your partner. Read your partner's letter, and mark any errors that you see.***

7. *Polish:* ***When you get your paper back, look for your partner's corrections. IMPORTANT: if you have any questions about grammar or spelling, ask the teacher before you hand in the letter. Then make any necessary changes.***

8. *Give your letter to the teacher.*

SAMPLE LETTER

June 31, 1994

Complaint Department
Acme Clothing Center
555 Bush St.
Metropolis, US 11101

Dear Sir or Madam:

I am writing to you about an item I bought at the Acme store on Bush Street last month, on May 15. I purchased a red wool pullover in the Women's Sportswear department, for $25.00. When I got home and unpacked the sweater, I found that there was a hole in the back.

On May 18 I took the sweater back to the return counter at the store. The counter person told me that he could not exchange the sweater for another, because they were out of stock. He told me he could not give me a refund of cash, either.

I am writing to complain about this purchase and to ask for my money back. I often shop at Acme, and I am usually satisfied. But I should not have to pay for a poorly-made item. Please advise me how to get a refund or an exchange.

Sincerely,

J. Rivers
1201 Center St.
Metropolis, US 11121

Unit 4 HOW MUCH DOES IT WEIGH?

WHOLE CLASS

PRESENTATION LET'S TALK ABOUT WEIGHTS

We need to talk about how much things weigh for many reasons.
Why do we need to know about weight in the following situations?

in a grocery store ______________________________

at the post office ______________________________

at the doctor's office ______________________________

at a hardware store ______________________________

When we talk about weighing solid things, we can use two kinds of measures. Most people around the world use grams (g) and kilograms (kg). Americans use ounces (oz) and pounds (lbs).

WHAT YOU NEED TO KNOW:

Solids:

8 ounces (8 oz) = a half pound (1/2 lb)
16 ounces (16 oz) = 1 pound (1 lb)
1 oz = 28.3 g
1 lb = 453 g
2.2 lbs = 1 kg

Liquids:

1 cup (cp) = 8 fluid ounces (8 fl. oz)
2 cps = 1 pint (pt)
2 pts = 1 quart (qt)
4 qts = 1 gallon (gal)
1 pt = 0.47 liters
1 qt = 0.95 liters

Answer the following questions:

1. How many ounces are there in a quarter pound (1/4 lb)? ________
2. How ounces are in 1 kilogram? ________
3. How many ounces does 100 grams weigh? __________
4. How much does 1 kilogram weigh in pounds? __________
5. How many liters are in 1 gallon? _______
6. How many quarts are in 1 liter? ______
7. How many cups are in 1 pint? ________
8. How many pints are in 1 quart? ______
9. How many quarts are in 1 gallon? ________
10. How many cups are in 1 gallon? ________

INTER ACTIVITY 1 USING A SCALE

WHAT YOU NEED TO BRING:

In groups of three people, find answers for the following questions by using the scale to measure some objects. One person puts the objects on the scale, another person reads the scale, a third person records the weight on paper, and each person takes turns reporting the results to the class, using complete sentences. Everyone helps in making the calculations.

1. *Write the name of each object and its weight in pounds and ounces as well as kilograms and grams:*

Object	Weight in pounds	Weight in ounces	Weight in kilograms	Weight in grams
________	______	______	______	______
________	______	______	______	______
________	______	______	______	______
________	______	______	______	______

Continue this activity on a separate piece of paper with additional objects.

Answer the following questions:

1. How much does the heaviest object weigh in ounces? ____________
2. How much does the second-heaviest object weigh in ounces? ____________
3. How much more does the heaviest object weigh than the second-heaviest object?______________ kg/g or ___________________________lbs/oz.
4. How much does the lightest object weigh?_____________________lbs/oz.

INTER ACTIVITY 2 COMPARING WEIGHTS

Each group picks two objects which look like they weigh the same. The groups weigh the two objects without telling other class members the results. The other class members try to guess which of the two objects weighs more. A reporter from the group tells the class how much more one object weighs than the other, using ounces and pounds.

Write the sentence of comparison: ______________________________

____

WHOLE CLASS PRESENTATION LET'S TALK ABOUT COUNTING

In the U.S., we use different terms to count certain objects. For instance, we say

a box of	cereal cookies detergent	for dry, solid things that come in a box;
a can of	soup peas dog food	for wet, liquid things that come in a can;

but we say

a head of lettuce, cabbage, or other leafy vegetables

a bunch of grapes, bananas, or fruits joined together

a pound of peppers, onions, apples, and coffee

a stalk of celery, **an ear of** corn, **a loaf of** bread

a pint of, **a quart of**, or **a gallon of** milk, juice, or other liquids

Fill in the blanks below:

1. a ____________ of crackers
2. a ____________ of juice
3. a ____________ of milk
4. a ____________ of onions
5. a ____________ of cauliflower
6. a ____________ of soda
7. a ____________ of cereal
8. a ____________ of cat food
9. a ____________ of ground beef
10. a ____________ of rice

INTERACTIVITY 3 FINDING PRICES AT THE SUPERMARKET

Find out the costs of the following items at your local supermarket. When you bring your list to class, compare it with those of students who went to other supermarkets. You may find some bargains!

Grocery Items		Your Store's Price	Another Store's Price
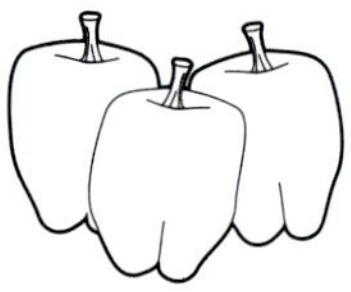	a pound of green peppers	________	________
	a quart of milk	________	________
	a bunch of bananas	________	________
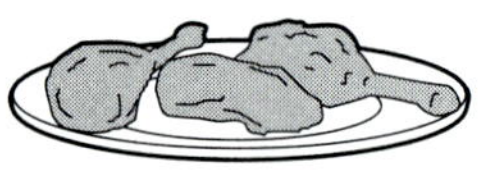	a pound of chicken	________	________
	a package of chocolate pudding	________	________
	a gallon of bottled water	________	________
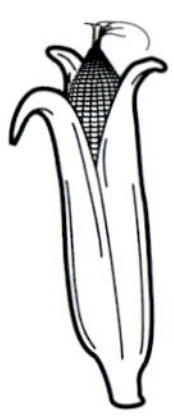	an ear of corn	________	________
	a loaf of white bread	________	________

ACTIVITY 4 UNIT PRICING

(INTER)

WHAT YOU NEED TO BRING:

Two empty boxes of different brands of the following items:

cereal	beans	rice	spaghetti	milk
cake mix	fruit juice	potato chips	cookies	crackers

Find out the price and write it on the box.

Many supermarkets offer shoppers a way to compare the costs of different brands of the items they sell. The system is called "unit pricing." In unit pricing, the store shows the cost of an item by the unit of weight.

WHAT YOU NEED TO KNOW:

PACKAGE PRICE ÷ NET WEIGHT = UNIT PRICE

product name	package price	net weight in oz	unit price
PEAS	$0.99	10 oz	$0.10 / oz

With your group, fill in the list below, using the packages you brought to class. Write the name of the product, the price of the package, the net weight in ounces, and the unit price. Write "X" next to the name of the product that has the lowest unit price.

Comparison Shopping List

Name of Product	Package Price	Weight in Ounces	Unit Price
1a. ________	________	________	________
1b. ________	________	________	________
2a. ________	________	________	________
2b. ________	________	________	________
3a. ________	________	________	________
3b. ________	________	________	________
4a. ________	________	________	________
4b. ________	________	________	________
5a. ________	________	________	________
5b. ________	________	________	________
6a. ________	________	________	________
6b. ________	________	________	________
7a. ________	________	________	________
7b. ________	________	________	________

INTER ACTIVITY 5 REPORTING ABOUT UNIT PRICES

1. In your group, write one sentence that reports on what you found in the Comparison Shopping List in InterActivity 4.

You may want to comment on what you found. For example, you may write,

"The larger packages often have a lower unit price."

Or you may write,

"The unit prices at my store are higher than at the other stores. I am surprised!"

When you have finished your sentence, pass it to one of the other students in your group. When you get a new paper with someone else's sentence, write your own comment. For example, if someone wrote one of the sentences above, you might write,

"The unit price is much lower in the larger packages,"

or you might write,

"I'm not surprised that things cost more at that store; they always have high prices!"

Be creative and write whatever you really feel!

____

____

____

____

____

____

____

2. When your group has finished, give your papers to the teacher.

INTER ACTIVITY 6 READ, WRITE, AND DISCUSS

Read the following paragraph as many times as you can in five minutes. After you have finished reading, cover the paragraph and write down what you can remember of it. Don't worry if you can't remember every word.

Andrew was so miserable that he would have cried, if he didn't know that eighth-grade boys never cry. The books in his backpack weighed down on him like huge stones. As he plodded slowly home, he thought to himself, "They must weigh forty pounds! But that can't be. My father told me that they only weigh a third of what I weigh, and half of what my brother weighs. And I weigh thirty-five pounds more than he does."

1. Write the meaning of the paragraph in your own words:

____

____

____

____

____

____

____

____

____

____

____

2. Answer these questions:

How much does Andrew weigh? ______________________________

How much does his brother weigh? ______________________________

3. Discuss your answers with the group.

WHOLE CLASS

PRESENTATION WRITING A RECIPE

One way that we commonly use weights and measures is in preparing food from a recipe. There are many books and magazines that have recipes we use in cooking. Many packages of food also contain recipes for the use of that item. But you can probably write out your own recipe that is not found in any book or on any package.

WHAT YOU NEED TO KNOW:

STEPS IN WRITING CLEARLY

1. BRAINSTORMING
2. DRAFTING
3. EDITING
4. PROOFREADING AND REWRITING
5. WRITING THE FINAL DRAFT

1. Brainstorm with your teacher. *Think of several different foods that you may want to cook. Make a list of four or five favorite recipes you can make. Keep your choices simple! Some people do not know how to cook as well as you do!*

____

____

____

____

2. Draft your recipe. *Take ten minutes and begin to write out your favorite recipe for something easy to cook. Focus on writing clear directions so that everyone will know how to cook your dish. When you go home tonight, finish the recipe, remembering to list all the ingredients and the quantities needed, as in the sample recipe on page 41. Bring your recipe to the next class meeting.*

Ingredients: ____

____

____

____

3. Edit your recipe in class. *Compare your recipe with the sample and with those of other students in the class. Remember: This is only a draft, so you should not worry if you make errors. You will have a chance to correct the errors before giving the final draft to the teacher.*

4. On a separate piece of paper, rewrite your recipe, and include all of the changes that you have made in class.

SAMPLE RECIPE

Here is a sample recipe for making cookies:

Ingredients:
2 1/4 cups of flour
3/4 cup of white sugar
3/4 cup of packed brown sugar
1 teaspoon baking soda
1 cup of butter
1 teaspoon vanilla extract
2 eggs
2 cups of chocolate bits and/or
1 cup chopped walnuts

Directions: Heat the oven to 375 degrees Fahrenheit. Then combine the flour, baking soda and salt. In a large bowl combine the butter, sugar, brown sugar, and vanilla extract. Beat them until they are smooth and creamy. Next add the eggs and continue beating. Slowly add in the flour mixture as you continue beating. Then stir in the chocolate bits and nuts. Last, take a tablespoon and drop spoonfuls of the batter onto a cookie sheet. Leave three inches between each spoonful. When the cookie sheet is full, bake it in the oven for about ten minutes. If you make the whole batter, you will get about 50 cookies.

To the Teacher: Here are some suggestions for further activities:

1. *Collect all the recipes into a book, and make photocopies for everyone in the class.*
2. *Vote on the best recipes, and ask the writers to bring their dishes to class for a party!*
3. *Exchange recipes with students from another class, and try out the recipes. Afterward, write letters to the makers of the recipes, thanking them or giving them some suggestions.*

Unit 5 HOW DOES YOUR MONEY GROW?

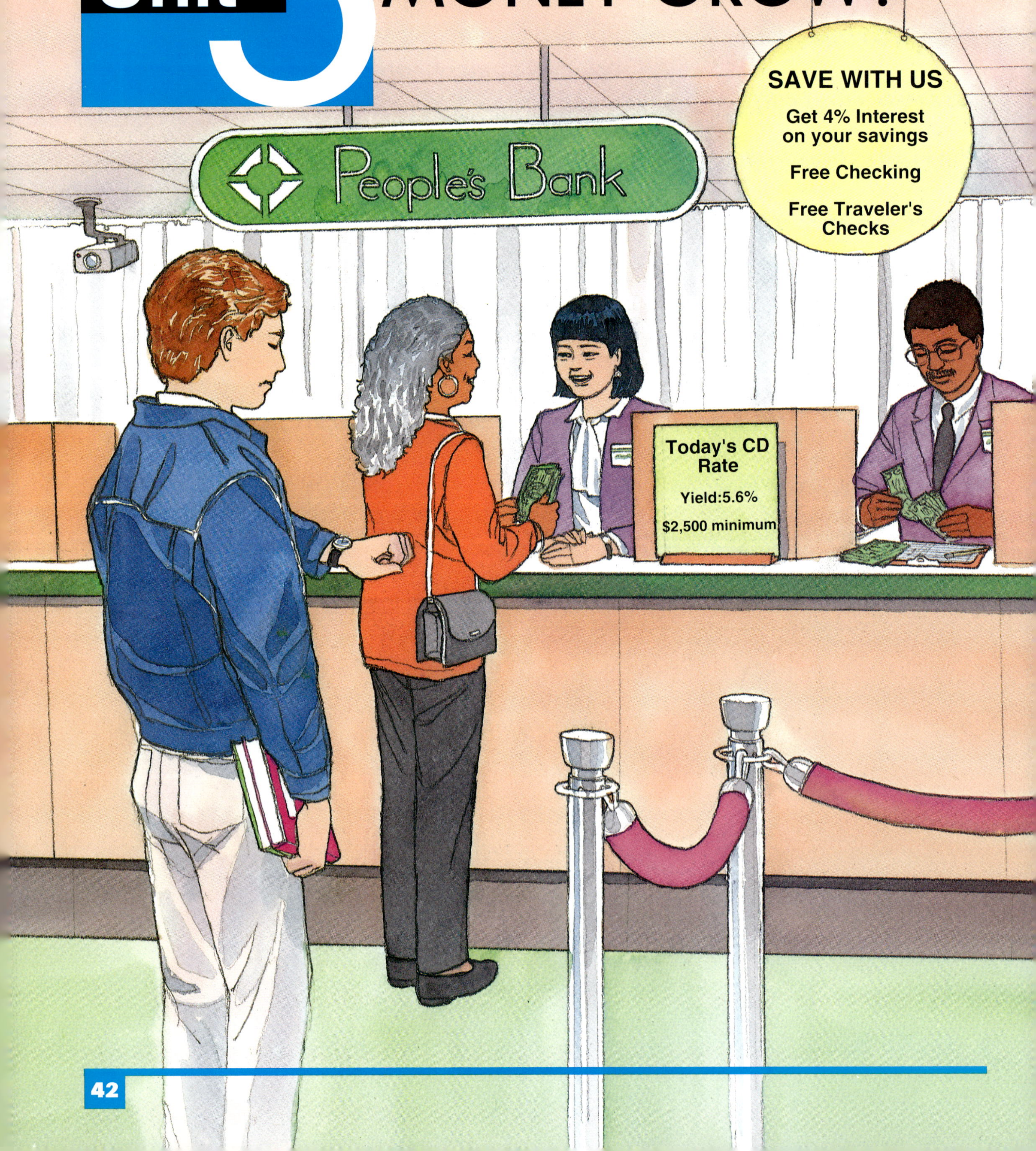

WHOLE CLASS

PRESENTATION LET'S TALK ABOUT MONEY

It is always important to know about money—how to get it, how to save it, and how to spend it. Getting money is always a problem, but it is not an easy one to solve. In this Unit, we will discover how to save money and how to spend some of it.

WHAT YOU NEED TO KNOW:

account = the money that you keep in a bank

deposit = put money into an account at a bank

withdraw = take money out of an account

interest = the money you earn on your account

savings bank = a bank that pays interest for money in savings accounts

Answer the following questions.

1. Look at the drawing on page 42. Where does this scene take place?____________

2. Who are the people in this picture? ____________

____

3. What do you think the woman is talking about with the teller? Write some of their conversation in the space below.

____

____

4. In the space below, write some of the reasons why people put money in banks.

____

____

____

5. Now, give some reasons why people withdraw money from banks.

____

____

____

INTER ACTIVITY 1 CHECKING ACCOUNTS

Some banks offer checking accounts to their customers who keep money in the bank. With a checking account, the customer may write checks to pay bills, instead of paying cash. With a partner, you are going to write out some checks to pay some bills.

WHAT YOU NEED TO KNOW:

check = a slip of paper to pay money from an account at a bank

checking account = the money that you keep in a bank to write checks against

check register = a list of the checks and amounts of money you deposited and withdrew from your checking account

1. Look carefully at the sample check below. You will see certain letters: (a), (b), (c), and so on.

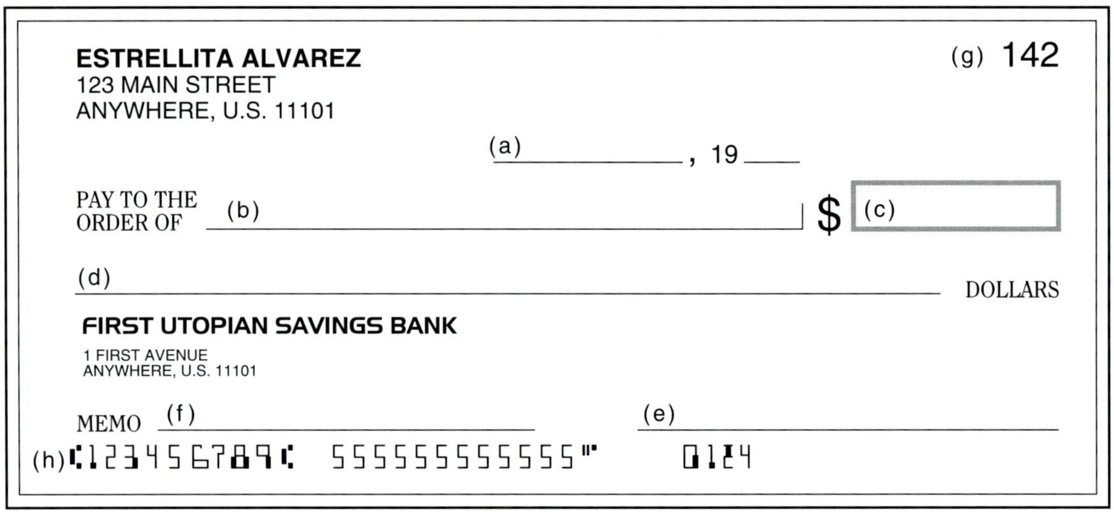

2. Now follow these steps:

1. Find (a). Put today's date in the space.
2. Find (b). Here is where you write the name of the company that will receive the money. Write "Big Bell" in this space.
3. Find (c). Here is the box where you write the amount of money in numbers. Write "$41.57" in this space.
4. Find (d). Here you write out the amount of money in words, but with numbers for the cents. Write "Forty-one and 57/100" in this space.
5. On line (e) you write your signature to show that you approve the check.

6. On line (f) you write the reason for the check—for example, "telephone bill."
7. Notice that (g) is the number of the check, in case you need to find the check later.
8. Notice also that (h) is the number of your account at the bank, which you will need to know for depositing money.

*3. After you have written the check, go to the check register. Enter the amount of the check under **AMOUNT PAID**, and subtract it from the balance, which is $1,000:*

$1,000 - $41.57 = $958.43.

*Write "$958.43" under **BALANCE**.*

CHECK REGISTER

19____ BE SURE TO DEDUCT ANY PER CHECK CHARGES OR MAINTENANCE CHARGES THAT MAY APPLY.

DATE		CHECK NUMBER	CHECKS ISSUED TO OR DEPOSIT RECEIVED FROM	AMOUNT DEPOSITED		✓ T	AMOUNT PAID		BALANCE	
									1,114.	37
8	23	139	The Barber Shop				20.	50	1,093.	87
8	24	140	The Home Market				70.	14	1,023.	73
8	24	141	Public Utilities				23	73	1,000.	00

4. Take the time to study this example carefully so that you are familiar with it.

5. With your group, list some good points and bad points of checking accounts.

INTERACTIVITY 2 MAKING YOUR OWN CHECKS

WHAT YOU NEED TO BRING:

paper

a pencil

With a partner, make your own checks, as follows:

1. On a separate piece of paper, draw three rectangles in the same shape as in InterActivity 1. In each rectangle, write in your name and address, "Pay to the order of," the name of the bank, and the numbers on the bottom of the check, just like the model in your book. When you have finished, cut the rectangles out of the paper, and you have your own "checks."

2. Imagine you have received a bill for $53.09 from the telephone company, called Big Bell. Write out a check in pencil that you might send. Don't forget to write yourself a note on the Memo line. When you finish, compare your check with your partner's check. Are they the same? Enter the new amount in the Check Register as you did in InterActivity 1. When you are satisfied that you did it correctly, take a new check and do step 3.

3. Write a check to your teacher for $101.45 (she or he deserves it!). On the Memo line, write "for services rendered," which means you are paying for work done. When you finish, go on to step 4.

4. Write a check payable to yourself for $15.44. When you write such a check, the bank will give you the money in cash at the teller window. Don't forget the Memo line (make up a reason why you need cash). When you receive a check made out to you, you must sign the check on the reverse side, at the top. Do that now. After you have signed the check, anyone can cash it, so be careful. To make sure the check is safe, write "For deposit only" and the number of your account under your signature.

INTER ACTIVITY 3 FIGURING OUT INTEREST

WHAT YOU NEED TO BRING:

paper

a pencil

a calculator (if possible)

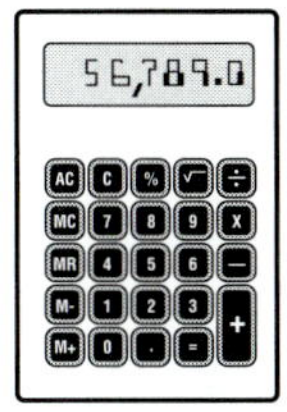

WHAT YOU NEED TO KNOW:

Principal = money that earns interest in a bank
Interest Rate = a percent (%) the bank pays you on your principal
Principal x Interest Rate = Interest

Here is a chart of principals and interest rates.

PRINCIPAL	x	INTEREST RATE	=	INTEREST
$1,000		5%		$50
$3,000		5%		________
$4,000		____		________
$5,000		____		________
$10,000		____		________

With a group, figure out what the interest will be if you put $3,000 or more in a bank at different interest rates for one year. Use the following steps:

a. **Estimate.** With your group, make a guess about the amount of interest you will earn if you deposit $3,000 in a savings account at a 5% interest rate.
b. **Figure out** the exact amount of interest at that rate.
c. **Write** the interest you have figured out in the **INTEREST** column.
d. **Start over** with a different interest rate for $4,000. With your group, decide on a new interest rate, guess the amount of interest, figure out the exact interest, and write the amount in the **INTEREST** column.
e. **Continue** for $5,000 and $10,000.

Now figure out how much interest you would earn if you left the money in the bank for a second year. Add the interest to the principal, and multiply the new amount by the interest rate. For example:

New Principal	x	Interest Rate	=	Interest
$1,000 + $50 = $1,050	x	5%	=	$52.50

This new interest is called ***compound interest.***

INTER ACTIVITY 4 A VISIT TO A SAVINGS BANK

Visit a savings bank near where you live. When you go there, ask to speak to a Customer Service Representative, someone whose job is to explain the bank's services. NOTE: Don't ask the teller to explain the services, because other people will be unhappy if you take too much time.

1. Find out the following information:

a. What is the current interest rate on savings accounts? ______________

b. What is the monthly service charge for checking accounts? ______________

c. What is the charge for money orders? ______________

d. What other important services does the bank provide?

Ask the Customer Service Representative any other questions you have, and remember to thank the person for helping you. If you are unable to get the information at a savings bank, you may study an advertisement for a savings bank, which may have some of the same information.

2. In your group, make a chart like the one below with information on the banks you visited.

NAME OF THE BANK	INTEREST ON SAVINGS	CHARGE FOR CHECKING ACCOUNTS	CHARGE FOR MONEY ORDERS	OTHER IMPORTANT SERVICES
______	______	______	______	______
______	______	______	______	______
______	______	______	______	______

3. In the opinion of your group, which of the banks on your chart is the best? Write the name of the bank, and the reasons for your choice, in the space below:

____

____

____

INTERACTIVITY 5 A REPORT ABOUT YOUR VISIT TO THE SAVINGS BANK

Write a short report about your visit to the savings bank. Use the answers to the questions in InterActivity 4 to help you. Remember, study an advertisement for a savings bank, if you need more information.

1. Begin your report this way:

At my nearby savings bank I learned a lot about interest on accounts, about the bank's services, and about the charges for these services.

___

___

___

___

___

___

___

___

___

___

___

___

2. When you have finished your draft, show it to a classmate or to your teacher to get comments about it, and make any changes you need to make.

3. Then rewrite the draft on a separate sheet of paper.

4. In class, proofread your draft with another student before handing it in to the teacher.

INTER ACTIVITY 6 OPINIONS ABOUT MONEY AND BANKS

Not everyone likes to use banks. Some people feel that banks are unreliable or that they may lose their money in a bank. Some people prefer to use cash for all their business transactions. Other people feel that carrying cash is dangerous, especially in large cities. They prefer to use banks for convenience and safety.

Form a group of five people with whom you have not worked before in this class. Complete the chart below for yourself, and then compare your answers with those of other people in your group.

1. Put a check (√) in the column that is closest to your opinion:

OPINIONS	Really disagree	Some doubt	No opinion	Some agreement	Really agree
1. A savings bank is a safe place to put my money.	_____	_____	_____	_____	_____
2. Paying bills by check is more convenient than by cash or money order.	_____	_____	_____	_____	_____
3. Carrying more than $25 in cash is dangerous.	_____	_____	_____	_____	_____
4. Using an ATM card to get money and pay for some items is convenient.	_____	_____	_____	_____	_____
5. I prefer to use a credit card instead of checks.	_____	_____	_____	_____	_____
6. Banks are too complicated; I don't want to get involved.	_____	_____	_____	_____	_____

2. Compare your answers with the answers of other people in your group.

3. Compare your group's answers with those of other groups. Which of the six opinions on the chart caused the most discussion?

INTERACTIVITY 7 REPORTING YOUR FINDINGS

Using the results of the survey in InterActivity 6, write a report about the preferences of the people in your group about using banks, cash, checks, and credit cards. To write the report, use the following steps:

1. *Brainstorm: With your group, select the opinion that got the most interesting reactions. Talk about why people reacted as they did. Be sure to write down what people say.*
2. *Organize: With a partner, decide on an order of presentation for your findings. List the reasons why people agree with the opinion; then list the reasons why people disagree. Write your reasons in the spaces below.*

Reasons to agree with the opinion:	Reasons to disagree with the opinion:
a. ________________	a. ________________
b. ________________	b. ________________
c. ________________	c. ________________
d. ________________	d. ________________

3. *Draft: Write a draft of your report on a separate piece of paper.*
4. *Pair-edit: Give your draft to your partner. Ask him or her to read your draft carefully and to tell you about any mistakes. As you read your partner's paper, make sure the paper says what your partner means to say. Mark with a pencil any parts of the paper that you think need changes, and return the draft.*
5. *Rewrite: Write your draft over again on a new piece of paper, this time including all the changes you made in the first draft.*
6. *Proofread: Before you submit the rewritten draft to the teacher, ask a partner to go over your paper with you carefully to see if you have made any grammar or spelling errors.*
7. *When you are satisfied with your draft, hand it in to the teacher.*

Unit 6 WHAT HAPPENED THEN?

B

A

D

C

WHOLE CLASS PRESENTATION LET'S TALK ABOUT TIME

In this Unit, we are going to look at ways of talking about time, and ways of telling about a series of things that happen. When we tell stories, report events, or give instructions, we need to tell about events as they occur in a time sequence.

1. Look at the pictures on the opposite page. The pictures show the events of a story. Write a short description of each picture:

____

____

____

____

____

____

2. Decide on the sequence of the pictures: which picture comes first in the story, which comes next, which comes later, and which one is last.

3. Write out the sequence of events in the story:

____

____

____

____

____

____

____

4. Tell your story to another student.

INTER ACTIVITY 1 USING TIME EXPRESSIONS

WHAT YOU NEED TO KNOW:

Some Time Expressions

a quarter to four	twenty after ten
half past eight	nine sharp
ten of two	a little before one
a quarter past five	high noon

1. With a partner, write the correct time expression under each clock face.

a. ______________ ______________

b. ______________ ______________

c. ______________ ______________

d. ______________ ______________

e. ______________ ______________

f. ______________ ______________

g. ______________ ______________

h. ______________ ______________

2. List other time expressions you have heard (for example: "around two," "five on the dot"):

____

____

____

3. With a group, discuss the meaning of these time expressions.

INTER ACTIVITY 2 FILL IN THE CLOCK HANDS

1. With a partner, draw clock hands which show the digital times below:

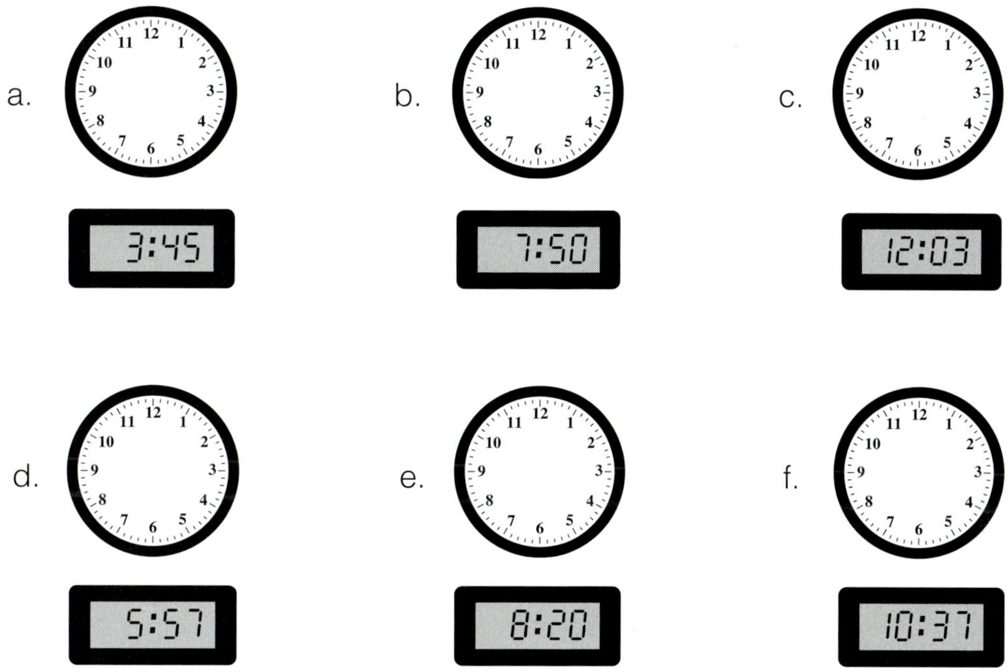

2. Write out the words describing each of these times:

a. ____________________

b. ____________________

c. ____________________

d. ____________________

e. ____________________

f. ____________________

3. Compare your answers made with those of others in your group.

4. Which type of clock, a or b, is easier for telling time? Why? Decide with your group. Write your answer below:

____

____

INTER ACTIVITY 3 CHOOSING A SEQUENCE

We often find that we need to do things in a certain order, or sequence, to do them well.

1. With a partner, study the following list of steps in sending a gift through the mail. Number the steps in the order you think is best.

Sending a Gift Through the Mail

____Give the package to the clerk, and pay the money for the postage.

____Write the receiver's name and address clearly on two sides of the package.

____Wrap the package in brown paper.

____Weigh the package to find out how much postage you will need.

____Use lots of packing material to protect fragile things.

____Take the package to the post office.

____Be sure to write your return address on the package.

____Put the gift inside a strong package.

____Seal the package carefully with strong tape.

2. Now with your partner, decide on your own sequence for one of the following tasks:

washing dishes ironing shirts changing a tire

3. Write your sequence in the space below:

____

____

____

____

4. When you have finished, share your sequence with others in your class.

INTERACTIVITY 4 ARRANGING EVENTS IN A SEQUENCE

Sometimes it is useful to note the time sequence of events. For example, suppose you lost something valuable to you, like a set of keys. You might try to remember where you lost them by recalling the sequence of things you did.

1. Look at the list of events on the day Rosa lost her library book.

Rosa's Day

5:00 p.m.	returned home, noticed the book was missing
9:30 a.m.	finished washing dishes
11:45 a.m.	met her friend Sally for lunch
8:10 a.m.	ate breakfast
3:00 p.m.	stopped for a snack, did not have the book
10:00 a.m.	visited the library, checked out a book
1:05 p.m.	took a bus downtown to shop, did not have the book
7:30 a.m.	woke up, washed her face, got dressed

2. With a small group, help Rosa find the book by writing the list of events in the correct order:

____

____

____

____

3. Decide when you think Rosa might have lost her book. What does your group think happened to Rosa's book?

____

____

4. Choose one person from the group to tell the rest of the class your answer.

INTER ACTIVITY 5 WRITING ABOUT A SEQUENCE OF EVENTS

After you have completed InterActivity 4, write a report with your group about the sequence of events that it describes. In your report, you can use some of the words below that show the sequence of events:

WHAT YOU NEED TO KNOW:

SEQUENCE WORDS

first	goes with the earliest event
second	goes with the event that followed the first
next, then, after that	go with later events
lastly, finally, in the end, at last	go with the last event in the sequence

1. Make your report about the sequence of events on the day Rosa lost her book. In your last sentence, tell when you think Rosa lost her book.

____

____

____

____

____

____

____

____

____

2. When you have finished your story, share it with the other students in your class.

INTER ACTIVITY 6 A PUZZLE FOR YOU

With a group, rewrite the following sentences in the correct order, with the boldface words arranged in a vertical row. If the sentences are in the correct order, the underlined words will form another sentence:

They told me that if I was **good** and waited for it, I might get it.

If someone promised me a gift, I said, "It **has** to come in a hurry; I can't wait!"

One day, I had seen a wonderful telescope in **its** own case.

When I was young, I wanted **everything** at once.

But as **time** passed, I got impatient; I forgot all about the telescope.

I told my parents I wanted it for my very **own**.

1. Rewrite the story in the space below:

___

___

___

___

___

___

___

___

___

2. Now read the parents' words by copying the boldface words in order:

___

INTER ACTIVITY 7 READ, WRITE, AND DISCUSS

All of us have been frightened at one time or another. When we are frightened, it seems that time moves very slowly, or even stops completely. Later, we can remember the sequence of events very clearly and can reconstruct it.

Read the following paragraph as many times as you can in five minutes. After you have finished reading, cover the paragraph and write down what you can remember of it. Don't worry if you can't remember every word.

"My Scariest Moment"

I'll never forget it; we almost drowned in a rental car. We were coming back from a dinner at a friend's house in Maui. There was a heavy January rainstorm, and the streets were flooded with deep puddles. To get home, we had to cross a short bridge, but it was under six inches of water when we got there, after midnight. We started slowly across, and then it happened: first we felt the car lift up off the road. Then the car turned and floated down a stream. Next we banged against the concrete walls of the stream. After that, the ocean waves began lifting the car and dropping it. That was when we thought we were going to die. Instead, we climbed out of the car through the windows and waded to shore, toward the flashlights of some onlookers. At last, we found a wonderful older couple who graciously let us sleep in their home overnight. I'll never forget that adventure—out to sea in a rental car!

1. Write down the meaning of the paragraph in your own words:

____

____

____

____

____

____

____

____

2. Compare your version of the story with a partner's version.

INTER ACTIVITY 8 MY SCARIEST MOMENT

In this InterActivity, you will write a report about your own scariest moment. Meet with a small group of students and trade stories. Make sure you tell all the details you can remember. Before you tell the story, write notes to help you remember what happened. To write the report, use the following steps:

1. *Brainstorm: With your group, decide what kinds of stories your group prefers. Make a list of all the details that are the scariest.*

2. *Organize: Write out a list of the events in the story in the spaces below. Remember to set up the story by telling what had happened before the story begins. Arrange the events in your story in the correct sequence, including all the important details:*

a. What had just happened before the story begins?

____

b. What happened first?

____

c. Then what happened?

____

d. And then?

____

e. After that?

____

f. Finally, what happened?

____

____

3. *Draft: Write a draft of your story on a separate piece of paper, and share it with members of your group. Ask them to read your draft aloud to you, so that you are certain you are saying what you mean. Make any necessary changes to clarify your meaning.*
4. *Rewrite: Write your draft over again, this time including all the changes you have made in the first draft.*
5. *Proofread: Before you give the rewritten draft to the teacher, ask a classmate to go over your paper with you, to see if you have made any grammar or spelling errors.*
6. *When you are satisfied with your final draft, hand it in to the teacher.*

Unit 7 ARE YOU PAYING MORE NOW?

PRESENTATION LET'S TALK ABOUT PRICE INCREASES

WHOLE CLASS

In this Unit we learn about how prices increase over a period of time.

Look at the pictures on the opposite page. The picture on top shows how much the average person spent on everyday things in the United States in 1980. Find out the following information from the picture on top, and write it in the column headed ***Price in 1980:***

Item:	Price in 1980	Price in 1990
a loaf of bread	________________	________________
a pound of beef	________________	________________
a quart of milk	________________	________________
a month's rent for an apartment	________________	________________
a ride on a city bus	________________	________________

Now look at the picture on the bottom of the page, and find out the prices of items in 1990. Write the prices in the column headed ***Price in 1990.***

Are there any other items that changed in price? In the spaces below, list the items which have increased in price since 1990, those that have not risen in price, and any that may have decreased in price.

a. Increased in Price:

____

____

b. Stayed the Same:

____

____

c. Decreased in Price:

____

____

INTER ACTIVITY 1 FIGURING OUT A PRICE INCREASE

WHAT YOU NEED TO BRING:

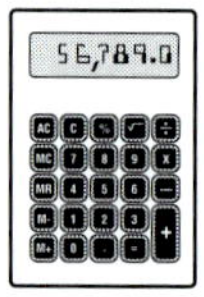

a calculator

WHAT YOU NEED TO KNOW:

$$\frac{\text{current price - past price}}{\text{past price}} \times 100 = \text{percent (\%) increase in price}$$

With a small group, find the percent increase in price for items in the list that you used in the Whole Class Presentation. Follow these steps:

a. Subtract the 1980 price of the item from the 1990 price.

b. Divide the number you found by the 1980 price. Use the calculator for this step. You will get a decimal number, like 0.25.

c. Multiply the decimal number by 100 (for example, 0.25 x 100 = 25%). This number is the percent increase for that item.

1. Write the percent increase for each item in the chart below.

Item	Percent Increase
a loaf of bread	______________
a pound of beef	______________
a quart of milk	______________
a month's rent for an apartment	______________
a ride on a city bus	______________

2. With your group, find out how much the prices of other items that you identified in the Whole Class Presentation have increased, and write them in the chart below. (Use a separate piece of paper if necessary.)

Item	Percent Increase
______________________	______________________
______________________	______________________
______________________	______________________

INTERACTIVITY 2 WORKING WITH TODAY'S PRICES

WHAT YOU NEED TO BRING:

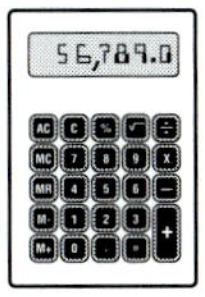

a calculator

With your group, compare the prices of 1990 with the prices that you pay today. Use the following steps:

a. Copy the 1990 price of each item in the column headed **Price in 1990** in the chart below. If possible, write the prices that you remember from 1990.

b. Find out today's price for each item, and write it under **Today's Price** in the chart.

c. Ask each member of the group to estimate the percent increase in price for these items.

d. Calculate the percent increase since 1990 for each item, as you did in InterActivity 1. Write it under **Percent Increase**.

e. Report your results to the rest of the class.

Item	Price in 1990	Today's Price	Percent Increase
a loaf of bread	________	________	________
a pound of beef	________	________	________
a quart of milk	________	________	________
a month's rent for an apartment	________	________	________
a ride on a city bus	________	________	________
a man's suit	________	________	________
a woman's dress	________	________	________
a pair of running shoes	________	________	________
a gallon of gasoline	________	________	________
a movie ticket	________	________	________

INTERACTIVITY 3 PRICES IN DIFFERENT COUNTRIES

Sometimes people think that prices, at least for some items, are much better in other countries. In this InterActivity, we will compare prices in two countries.

WHAT YOU NEED TO BRING:

a calculator

information about another country's prices and exchange rates

WHAT YOU NEED TO KNOW:

Exchange Rate: The amount of one country's money that you need to buy a certain amount of another country's money.

Here are some exchange rates in U.S. dollars:

1 Mexican peso = $0.32 U.S. dollars
1 Hong Kong dollar = $0.13 U.S. dollars
100 Japanese yen = $0.89 U.S. dollars

Price (in Country A)	x	Exchange Rate (for Country B)	=	Converted Price (Country B's $)

1. With a small group, compare the prices you have identified in InterActivitiy 2 with prices for similar items in another country. Use the following steps:

a. Choose two countries for comparison. For example, if the country we used in InterActivity 2 was the United States, we might choose Mexico and the United States as our countries for comparison. We then write "Mexico" next to COUNTRY A and "United States" next to COUNTRY B on the chart on page 67.

b. Under the column headed **PRICE,** write the current price in that country for each item listed on the chart. For example, if a loaf of bread costs 3 pesos in Mexico, we write "3 pesos" under PRICE.

c. Now we need to find the Exchange Rate for the countries we chose. For example, if today 1 Mexican peso = $0.32 U.S. dollars, we write "$0.32 U.S. dollars" under EXCHANGE RATE on the chart.

d. To be able to compare prices, we need to convert our prices for Country A into Country B's money. To do this, we multiply the price for each item in Country A by the Exchange Rate.

To continue our example, if the price for a loaf of bread is 3 Mexican pesos, then

Price	x	Exchange Rate	=	Converted Price
3 Pesos	x	$0.32	=	$0.96 U.S. dollars

We write "$0.96" under **CONVERTED PRICE**.

e. Now we are ready to compare. With your group, take the prices from InterActivity 2. Compare them with the prices under **CONVERTED PRICE (Country B's $)**.

PRICE COMPARISON CHART

COUNTRY A: ______________________ COUNTRY B: ______________________

ITEM	PRICE (Country A)	x	EXCHANGE RATE	=	CONVERTED PRICE (Country B's $)
a loaf of bread	________		________		________
a pound of beef	________		________		________
a quart of milk	________		________		________
a man's suit	________		________		________
a woman's dress	________		________		________
a pair of running shoes	________		________		________
a gallon of gasoline	________		________		________
a month's rent for an apartment	________		________		________
a ride on a city bus	________		________		________
a movie ticket	________		________		________

2. Which country's prices are better? For which items? How do you explain the differences? Write your ideas below:

____

____

____

____

INTER

ACTIVITY 4 UNDERSTANDING A CHART

WHAT YOU NEED TO BRING:

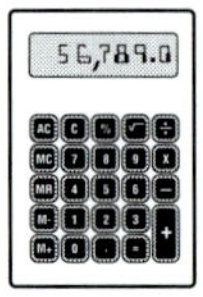

a calculator

WHAT YOU NEED TO KNOW:

$$\frac{\text{New Salary - Old Salary}}{\text{Old Salary}} \times 100 = \text{Percent (\%) Increase in Salary}$$

Average employee earnings, weekly, in U.S. dollars

Kinds of Workers	1988 Salary	1989 Salary
Electrical	409.25	418.24
Food products	367.54	383.35
Clothing	221.30	230.48
Chemical	533.40	553.24
Construction	500.26	518.54
Retail sales	188.40	194.05
Hotel and tourism	203.50	210.27
Legal services	446.25	483.21

1. With a group, study the chart above, and answer the following questions:

a. In 1989, which workers earned more, chemical workers or electrical workers?

____

b. In 1989, which workers earned more, retail sales workers or hotel and tourism workers?

____

c. How much more money did construction workers earn in 1989 than in 1988? (Hint: Subtract the number for 1988 from the number for 1989.)

____

d. How much more did hotel and tourism workers earn in 1989 than in 1988?

____

e. Of all the workers in the chart, which ones had the greatest increase in salary from 1988 to 1989?

____

f. What was the percent increase in salary for construction workers from 1988 to 1989?

____

INTER ACTIVITY 5 READ, WRITE, AND DISCUSS

Read the following passage as many times as you can in five minutes. After you have finished reading, cover the passage and write down what you can remember of it. Don't worry if you can't remember every word. At the end, add a sentence giving your own opinion.

Inflation is the name we use for price increases.

A popular measure of inflation in a country is called the Consumer Price Index, or CPI. In the United States, the CPI rose from 100 to 126 in the years 1985 to 1991. That means that prices rose 26% in those six years, or about 4% each year. At the same time, the hourly earnings index rose from 100 in 1985 to 117 in 1991. That means that workers earned 17% more in 1991 than in 1985, or about 3% more each year.

The prices rose faster than the earnings in those years. Even though workers earned more money, they could afford to buy less. What do you think about this situation?

1. Write the meaning of the passage in your own words.

____

____

____

____

____

____

____

____

____

____

____

____

2. Compare your answer with the answers of the others in your group.

INTER ACTIVITY 6 REPORTING ABOUT INFLATION

WHAT YOU NEED TO BRING:

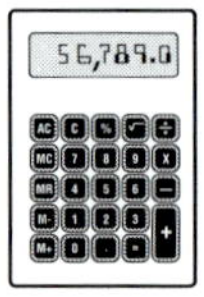

a calculator

Write a report about inflation in recent years. Follow these steps:

1. *Brainstorm: From the chart, choose three kinds of workers (for example, electrical workers, clothing workers, and construction workers). Find the percent increase in salary for each of the three kinds of workers you choose.*

Average employee earnings, weekly, in U.S. dollars

Electrical	376.91	430.80
Food products	342.86	398.75
Clothing	205.98	249.87
Chemical	479.13	598.12
Construction	469.38	538.86
Retail sales	180.58	204.92
Hotel and tourism	176.18	217.93
Legal services	364.00	506.81

2. *Organize: With a partner, work out an order of presentation of your findings. Report on the earnings of the three kinds of workers, and compare the increases in earnings with the 26% increase in prices. Use the chart below for your outline:*

Main point: ____

____

Supporting evidence: Percent increase in weekly salary

Kind of worker ____

Kind of worker ____

Kind of worker ____

26% increase in prices: Consumer Price Index (from InterActivity 5)

____

3. *Draft:* *Write a draft of your report in the space below:*

____

____

____

____

____

____

____

____

____

____

____

____

____

4. *Pair-edit:* *Give your draft to your partner. Ask him or her to read your draft carefully and to ask you about any mistakes. As you read your partner's paper, make sure that it says what your partner means to say. Mark with a pencil any parts of the paper that you think need changes, and return the draft to your partner.*

5. *Rewrite:* *Write your draft over again on a separate piece of paper, this time including all the changes you made in the first draft.*

6. *Proofread:* *Before you submit the rewritten draft to the teacher, ask a partner to go over your paper with you to see if you have made any grammar or spelling errors.*

7. *When you are satisfied with your draft, hand it in to the teacher.*

Unit 8 WHAT'S ON TV?

PRESENTATION LET'S TALK ABOUT TELEVISION

WHOLE CLASS

All over the world, television has become a major part of our lives. These days, people may spend several hours each day watching television. Some people think that the programs we see on television affect the way we live. In this Unit, we will explore how the class feels about television.

Look at the picture on the opposite page. Answer the following questions:

1. In this family of four people, how many are watching television? ____________

2. What kind of program do you think they are watching? ____________

____

3. When do you think this scene takes place—morning, afternoon, or evening?

____

4. Why do you think so? ____________

____

5. How many hours each day does your family watch television? ____________

6. What kinds of programs are your favorites? ____________

____

____

7. In your home, does everyone agree on the programs to watch, or do some people like to watch certain kinds of programs?

____

8. Do some family members like to watch certain programs? Which programs? ____________

____

____

INTER ACTIVITY 1 COUNTING THE SHOWS ON TV

*With a group, look at the chart below. It is a listing of all the television programs offered in a certain city on one evening. Count the number of shows offered for each category listed, and write the number under **How Many?** on the next chart. Under **Examples**, include the names of some shows in each category.*

	7:00	7:30	8:00	8:30	9:00	9:30	10:00
1	**Graham /Tyler News Hour** 60 Min.		**God's Green Acre** Gardening - 60 Min.		**Money Matters** Advice on Investing - 60 Min.		**In Our Capital** Political Coverage
2	**News** Local Coverage	**Rock News** Music News	**Around it Goes** Game Show	**What's New?** Gossip	**Police Files** Crime	**Many Moons** Comedy	**All Ashore** Comedy
3	**News** National Coverage	**Luck of the Draw** Game Show	**Monster form the Deep** Adventure Movie - 2 Hours				**The Search** Drama - 2 Hours
4	**News** Local Coverage	**News** Local Coverage	**My Brother Bob** Comedy	**Dark Journey** Romance	**Sky Hawk** Adventure	**Marking Time** Drama	**Last One Out** Drama
5	**Sports Line** 60 Min.		**Soccer** Bridgetown Bombers vs Edgewood Lions				**Score Time** Sports wrap-up
6	**Fortune Fantasy!** Game Show	**$10,000 Answer** Game Show	**The Underwater World** Documentary - 60 Min.		**Nature's Theater** Documentary - 60 Min.		**Family Forum** Discussion
7	**TV Shopper** Best Buy Hour - 60 Min.		**Bargain Time** Shoppers Call in - 60 Min.		**Be Slim Without Sweat** Paid Advertisement		**Workout with Tim** Exercise Program

Type of Show	How Many?	Examples
a. News or information	______	______________________________
b. Drama	______	______________________________
c. Adventure, crime, or mystery	______	______________________________
d. Comedy	______	______________________________
e. Sports	______	______________________________
f. Game	______	______________________________

1. Which of these shows do you think you would like to watch during the hours of 7 to 10 p.m.?

____

2. Which shows do you think your family would like to watch during these hours?

____

____

3. Compare your answers with those of other people in your group.

INTER ACTIVITY 2 FINDING OUT ABOUT TV TODAY

WHAT YOU NEED TO BRING:

a copy of the television schedule for this day

1. With a group, study the television listing on this day. Find out the numbers of different kinds of television programs that are offered on this day, and write them in the chart below.

2. Add any other types of shows on the lines at the bottom.

Type of Show	5 p.m. to 7 p.m.	7 p.m. to 10 p.m.
a. News or information	______	______
b. Drama	______	______
c. Adventure, crime, or mystery	______	______
d. Comedy	______	______
e. Sports	______	______
f. Game	______	______
______	______	______
______	______	______

3. Answer the following questions.

a. Which shows do you think adults would like to watch? ______

b. Teenagers? ______

c. Children? ______

d. Which kinds of shows does your group think are the most popular from 5 to 7 p.m.?

______

e. From 7 to 10 p.m.? ______

INTERACTIVITY 3 REPORTING YOUR FINDINGS

1. In the space below, make a report of the information you found in InterActivity 2.

2. In your report, be sure to answer the following questions:

a. What kinds of television shows appear most often during the hours of 5 to 7 p.m. in your city? Which kinds of shows appear most often between 7 and 10 p.m.?

b. Among the people in your group, which shows are the most popular?

c. In the opinion of your group, which shows do adults like to watch? Which shows do teenagers like to watch? Which shows do children like to watch?

____

____

____

____

____

____

____

____

____

____

____

____

3. Now share your report with your group. Compare results. You may want to make some changes in your report.

4. When you are satisfied that each report is complete, group members can share their reports with the other people in your class.

INTER ACTIVITY 4 HOW MUCH TV IS TOO MUCH?

Do you think that people watch too much television these days? Do you think they watch the wrong kinds of shows? In this InterActivity, we will find out opinions about TV.

1. Complete the chart below by giving your responses to the statements about watching TV.

Statements	I Agree	I'm Not Sure	I Disagree
a. There are too many crime shows on TV.	_______	_______	_______
b. There are not enough news and information shows.	_______	_______	_______
c. There is too much violence on TV at times when children watch.	_______	_______	_______
d. There are too many sports programs.	_______	_______	_______
e. There are not enough high-quality programs.	_______	_______	_______
f. There are too few programs in my native language.	_______	_______	_______
(Add your own statements.)			
____________________	_______	_______	_______
____________________	_______	_______	_______

2. When you have completed the chart, compare your responses with those of the other people in your group.

3. Add up all the responses for each statement, and find out how your group feels about the proper amount of television watching and the shows we should watch.

4. Discuss the reasons why you responded the way you did. As you discuss the responses, write down what people say about them on a separate piece of paper.

INTERACTIVITY 5 WRITING ABOUT TV PREFERENCES

1. *In the space below, write a paragraph in which you tell how your group responded to the statements in InterActivity 4.*

2. *In your paragraph, be sure to tell how the group responded to each of the statements.*

3. *Tell what comments people made about the quality of programs on television.*

4. *When you have finished your paragraph, show it to the others in your group, and make sure you have reported their comments accurately.*

5. *When you are sure that your paragraph is accurate, show it to your teacher. (You may want to copy it on a separate piece of paper.)*

INTER ACTIVITY 6 READ, WRITE, AND DISCUSS

Read the following passage as many times as you can in five minutes. After you have finished reading, cover the reading passage and write down what you can remember of it. Don't worry if you can't remember every word.

In the fifty years since television first appeared, it has grown to become one of the most powerful forces in influencing people. In many countries around the world, most families have a television set and watch it several hours each day. The programs that people watch are often their most direct source of news, information, and entertainment—not only about local events, but also about worldwide events. Television has made our world a "global village."

But television is also a source of controversy. Some people say that we watch too much television. Some say that there is too much crime shown on television. Some say that there are not enough high-quality programs. Many people fear that the programs on television that are designed for children contain too much violence and that such programs lead children to act violently.

But television is expanding rapidly. Soon there will be hundreds of programs available to viewers all over the world. Many people wonder whether we can use television as a tool for learning and communication or if, instead, it will ruin our lives.

1. Write down the meaning of the passage in your own words:

___

___

___

___

___

___

___

___

___

2. When you finish, show your paragraph to your teacher.

INTER ACTIVITY 7 WRITING A LETTER TO A TV STATION

Managers of TV stations are very interested in what their viewers think about TV programs. If enough people write to the station, the programs can be changed. In this activity, we will write letters to a local TV station and express our feelings about its programs.

1. Brainstorm: *With a group, discuss what you would like to say to a local station manager about the programs on TV. You may want to say*

a. that there is too much violence in children's programs.

b. that there is not enough sports.

c. that there should be more programs in your native language on the station.

In the space below, write down some of the opinions expressed in class about TV programs. Decide which ideas are important to you.

____

____

____

____

2. Draft: *When you have a good idea of what you want to say to the station manager, write a draft of a letter. Be sure to include today's date and the name and address of the station, as shown on page 81.*

3. Pair-edit and rewrite: *After you have written your draft, show it to a partner, who will read it over. When you get your partner's paper, read it carefully to make sure that you understand every sentence. If there are some parts that you do not understand, draw a circle around those parts, and discuss them with your partner. When you get your own paper back, make any necessary changes, and rewrite the letter on a separate piece of paper.*

4. Proofread: *Proofread your paper for sentence-level errors.*

5. *When the letter is ready, hand it in to your teacher.*

Letter Format

Today's Date: ______________________________

Station Manager's Name: ____________________

Name of the Station: _______________________

Address of the Station: ____________________

____

Dear ____________________:

I would like to tell you something about the programs on your station. _________

____

____

____

____

____

____

____

____

____

Sincerely,

Your Name: ______________________________

Your address: ____________________________

____

Unit 9 WHICH ONES BELONG TOGETHER?

WHOLE CLASS

PRESENTATION LET'S CLASSIFY

Every day we are faced with the task of classifying things and people. As you see in the picture on the opposite page, even when we do laundry, we must think about putting similar things together. When we want to tell others about our classifications, we have to make accurate descriptions.

Look at the picture on the opposite page and answer the following questions:

1. How many piles of folded clothes are on the table, and what does each pile contain?

____

____

2. Now look at the pile of unsorted clothes on the washing machine. It contains soiled clothes for washing. There are white cotton shirts, colored polyester shirts and blouses, cotton pants, and other clothes made of polyester fabrics.

a. What is the best way to sort the clothes for washing? ______________________

____

b. Give some good reasons for your choice: ______________________

____

c. What would happen if we washed all the clothes together? ______________________

____

d. What settings should we use on the washing machine with each different group of clothes?

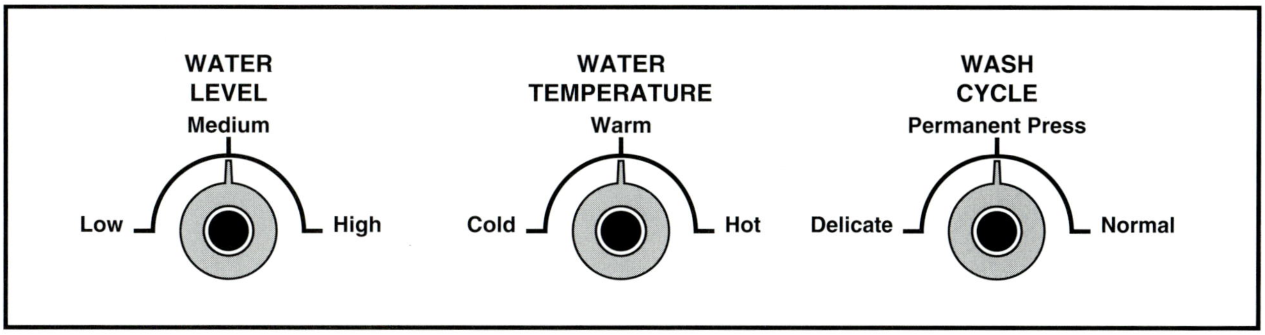

Which settings should we use for cotton clothes? ______________________

For permanent-press shirts and blouses? ______________________

For delicate fabrics, like silk? ______________________

INTER ACTIVITY 1 GIVING INSTRUCTIONS

1. *With a small group of your classmates, decide on instructions for washing a pile of clothes containing the following items:*

two white shirts	three nylon blouses	a wool sweater
five pairs of men's socks	three pairs of panty hose	a soiled work shirt
two pairs of jeans		

Remember to be specific about the amount of detergent, the water level, the temperature of the water, and the wash cycle on the washing machine.

2. *When you have decided on the instructions, write them out in the space below, and share them with other groups in the class.*

____

____

____

____

____

3. *Now let's write some instructions about drying the clothes in a clothes dryer.*

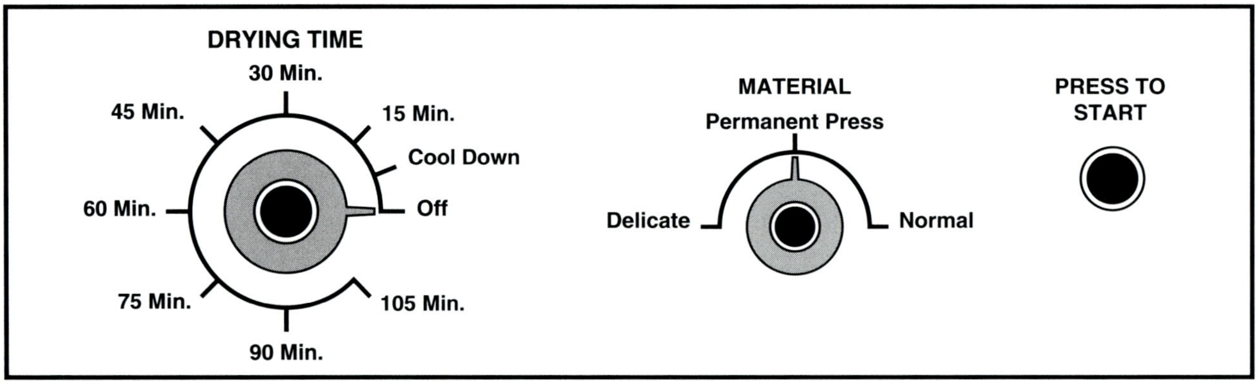

Decide with your group how to tell another group to dry the clothes. For example, you might say

"Put the clothes made of cotton in the dryer for half an hour."

____

____

____

INTER ACTIVITY 2 "SORTING OUT" FAMOUS PEOPLE

Sometimes it is useful to "sort out" people, also. Below are some noteworthy people and their accomplishments. See if you can match the people with their accomplishments by using sentences like

"Martin Luther King is the man who led the civil rights movement in the U.S."

1. Write the letter of the person in the space next to that person's accomplishments.

People	Accomplishments
a. Abraham Lincoln	___ worked for peace in the Middle East
b. Paul McCartney	___ led a protest for civil rights
c. Margaret Thatcher	___ freed slaves in America
d. Nelson Mandela	___ was President of the U.S. in 1994
e. Gloria Estefan	___ was once a Beatle, is still famous
f. Anwar Sadat	___ is a rock performer from Miami
g. Mother Teresa	___ was Britain's first woman Prime Minister
h. William Jefferson Clinton	___ worked with sick and homeless people

2. In your group, now classify these people by their work; that is, write each person's name under the correct heading.

Human Rights Leaders	Entertainers	National Leaders
______________	______________	______________
______________	______________	______________
______________	______________	______________
______________	______________	______________
______________	______________	______________

3. Extend the lists in part 2 with the names of other human rights leaders, entertainers, and national leaders.

4. With your group, now think of at least two other headings for classifying the people in your extended lists. (For example, "Men," "Women," "People from Africa," "People from North America.")

WHOLE CLASS

PRESENTATION HOW TO CLASSIFY YOURSELF

People think about themselves in different ways. For example, they might think about who they are, what they do for a living, or where they live.

Think of three words or phrases that describe who you are, what you do, and where you live. For example, if you are a bookkeeper who lives downtown with his children, you might write

father	bookkeeper	live downtown

or, you might write

rock music fan	mechanic	live in an apartment
stamp collector	factory worker	live with my parents

Put your phrases at the top of the columns on the chart below. Then, find up to four classmates who are in the categories you have made. For example, you might ask "Are you a bookkeeper?" "Do you live downtown?" List names under the headings.

Who You Are:	What You Do:	Where You Live:
______	______	______
______	______	______
______	______	______
______	______	______
______	______	______

1. When you have completed your chart, show it to other class members. Compare charts to see if you have some of the same people's names as others have.

2. What were some of the headings other people used to describe themselves? In the space below, write some of the headings you remember:

______

______

______

INTERACTIVITY 3 SORTING OUT PEOPLE IN YOUR CLASS

Form a group of people who used the same word to describe themselves. For example, you might form a group of tennis players. Make sure there are at least three people in your group. Then do the following activities:

a. Each person makes a list of other things they like to do. Compare your new list of interests with those of others in your group.

b. Give your group a name, and design a badge for the group.

c. Introduce the members of your group to the rest of the class. Be sure to mention the other interests they have told about.

d. On a separate piece of paper, write a paragraph describing the members of your group.

INTERACTIVITY 4 HOW DO YOU SPEND YOUR LEISURE TIME?

1. Write a list of three ways that you spend your leisure time.

2. Form a new group of people, one from each of the groups in InterActivity 3.

In this new group, find out how the people in your group spend their leisure time. Make a list of the activities each person does. For example, you may find one person, Joanna, who does many things: reads, takes walks, rides a bicycle, plays soccer, listens to music, does volunteer work. Write the list of everything that person does below his or her name:

Name:	Name:	Name:	Name:
Joanna	______	______	______
reads	______	______	______
takes walks	______	______	______
rides a bicycle	______	______	______
plays soccer	______	______	______
listens to music	______	______	______
does volunteer work	______	______	______

Use another sheet of paper if you need more space.

3. When you have found the leisure-time interests of your own group, report those interests to the rest of the class.

INTER ACTIVITY 5 FORMING AN INTEREST GROUP

1. Form a small group of people in your class who have similar leisure interests.

2. Interview the other members of the group to find the answers to the following questions:

a. When did you first start getting interested in this activity? ______________________

____

b. Why do you like this activity? ____

____

c. What special concerns or problems do we have to know about before doing this activity?

____

____

d. What is the best way to get started doing this activity? ________________________

____

____

e. What are the benefits of this activity? ______________________________________

____

____

3. When you have finished interviewing the others in your group, make a summary of all their answers by writing the answers on a separate piece of paper.

4. Give an oral report of the results of your interviews to the rest of the class.

INTERACTIVITY 6 WRITING A SUMMARY REPORT

1. With a partner from the group you formed in InterActivity 5, write a short summary report of what you found in your interviews. Use the following steps:

a. Look at your notes, and make sure that you have responses from each of the group members to all the questions.

b. Write a paragraph in which you make a summary of the answers to each question. For example, you might write

> "Our group found that we have all been interested in riding bicycles since we were children."

c. Sometimes your group will not agree on the responses to the questions. When that happens, you need to report the different reactions, for example:

> "Some of us think that it is easy to learn to ride a bicycle, but others think it is difficult, especially for adults."

d. Try to end your paragraph with an invitation for others to participate in your activity. For example:

> "Bicycle riding is a healthy sport. We hope everyone will join us."

____

____

____

____

____

____

____

____

____

____

2. When you and your partner finish writing your report, share it with the others in the group for their comments, and then share it with the whole class.

INTER ACTIVITY 7 REPORTING ABOUT YOUR CLASS

Using the results of the interviews about favorite leisure-time activities, write a report about the leisure-time activities of the people in your class. To write the report, use the following steps:

1. Brainstorm: *With a partner, sort the leisure-time activities into at least two categories—for example, team sports and individual sports, or indoor activities and outdoor activities. The categories are up to you to choose.*

Talk about why people liked their leisure activities, how to get involved in the activities, and any possible problems. Write your answers to these questions in the chart below:

Leisure-Time Activities in Our Class

Questions:	First Category (for example, team sports):	Second Category (for example, individual sports):	Third Category (your choice):
Which activities are included in this category?	________ ________ ________	________ ________ ________	________ ________ ________
What more would we like to learn about these activities?	________ ________ ________	________ ________ ________	________ ________ ________
How do we get involved in these activities?	________ ________ ________	________ ________ ________	________ ________ ________
Are there any problems we should know about?	________ ________ ________	________ ________ ________	________ ________ ________

2. Organize: *With your partner, decide how to present your findings. Remember that you want to report on the whole class, not just on your own group. Make a list of the different activities, the reasons that people like to do them, and what you want to learn more about.*

3. Draft: *Write a draft of your report in the space below. Begin like this:*

In our class we have several leisure-time interest groups.

____

____

____

____

____

____

____

____

____

____

____

4. Pair-edit: *Give your draft to your partner. Ask him or her to read your draft carefully and to ask you about any mistakes. As you read your partner's paper, make sure the paper says what your partner means to say. Mark with a pencil any parts of the paper that you think need changes, and return the draft to the writer.*

5. Rewrite: *Write your draft over again on a separate piece of paper, this time including all the changes you made in the first draft.*

6. Proofread: *Before you submit the rewritten draft to the teacher, ask a partner to go over your paper with you to see if you have made any grammar or spelling errors.*

7. *When you are satisfied with your draft, hand it in to the teacher.*

Unit 10 WHICH IS BETTER?

WHOLE CLASS

PRESENTATION LET'S COMPARE RADIOS

We all go shopping sometimes, and we all are interested in finding the most value for our money. In this Unit, we are going to make comparisons to find out the best quality for the least cost, for both products and places. At the end, we want to report our findings to our friends so they can share what we have found out.

Examine the picture of two portable radios shown on the opposite page. You will see that both of the radios have some features in common, but that there are also some differences.

Something special about an appliance is called a "feature." For example, a feature of a radio might be that it has powerful speakers, or that it has good sound. Write the features that both radios have in the first column. Write the special features that Radio A has in the second column. Write the special features for Radio B in the third column.

Both radios have:	Only Radio A has:	Only Radio B has:
______________	______________	______________
______________	______________	______________
______________	______________	______________
______________	______________	______________
______________	______________	______________
______________	______________	______________

Answer the following questions:

1. Which special features does Radio A have? ______________________________

____

2. Which special features does Radio B have? ______________________________

____

3. What is the cost of Radio A? ____________ Radio B? ______________________

4. Which radio do you think offers the best value? ______________________

5. Why do you think so? ______________________________________

INTER ACTIVITY 1 LOOKING AT NEWSPAPER ADS

WHAT YOU NEED TO BRING:

current copies of several daily newspapers

a pair of scissors

a marking pen

1. With your group, look through the newspapers to find advertisements for televisions, radios, or other appliances at local stores.

a. Form groups according to product.

b. Decide on one appliance for comparison of features and prices.

c. Draw a circle around each ad for the same type of appliance, so you can find it again easily.

2. Make a list of desirable features of each appliance, as follows:

Fill in the blank spaces in the chart below, listing the features for each appliance. Try to find ads for different brand names of the same size of appliance. For example, if you are looking for televisions, make sure that they all have the same size screen.

Brand name:	Brand name:	Brand name:
____________	____________	____________
Special features	Special features	Special features
____________	____________	____________
____________	____________	____________
____________	____________	____________
____________	____________	____________
____________	____________	____________
Price	Price	Price
____________	____________	____________

3. Compare the three advertisements, and decide which one offers the best value. Explain your conclusion to the other students in your class.

INTER ACTIVITY 2 MAKING YOUR OWN ADVERTISEMENT

WHAT YOU NEED TO BRING:

pictures of items taken from magazines and newspapers

pencils and marking pens

paste or glue

construction paper in several colors

With your group, decide on one item for which you will make an advertisement. For example, you may choose running shoes, makeup, cars, or soft drinks. Choose your item from among the pictures which you found in newspapers and magazines.

1. Use these steps in making your ad:

a. Choose a new name for your item, and decide what you want to say about the item. Remember to talk about the features and how they make the product better.

b. On a piece of construction paper, write a headline in large, bold letters. The headline should attract attention by saying something surprising.

c. In smaller letters, write two brief sentences (called "copy") that tell why this item is better than other brands. You may want to revise your headline and sentences several times so you can make your ad as attractive as possible.

d. When you have finished editing the ad, start with a fresh piece of construction paper, and place the picture, the headline, and the copy exactly where you want them. Use glue or paste to hold everything in position. You may want to draw in some graphic designs to make the ad complete.

2. When you have finished, display your ad to your classmates, and tell why you think your item is better than other brands.

WHOLE CLASS

PRESENTATION LET'S COMPARE PLACES

In some ways, choosing a place to live is like choosing a product to buy. We choose places by finding out the features that are best for us. Suppose you were advising a friend coming to live in North America. One question he would probably ask is "Where is it better to live?" Let's see if we can find out how to answer this question.

WHICH CITY DO YOU LIKE BEST?

A. Marlo Park, CA
Population: 60,000
Schools: many good public and private.
Employment: some industrial jobs, many technical and professional jobs.
Housing: mainly single-family homes; average cost: $1,500/month.
Cultural events: not many local events, but 30 miles from two large cities.
Ethnic communities: European-Americans.

B. Collegetown, TX:
Population: 125,000
Schools: some good private schools. Public schools: average.
Employment: fast growth in technical jobs, slow growth in industrial and service jobs.
Housing: single-family homes and apartments; average cost: $800/month.
Cultural events: some pop concerts, local theater groups.
Ethnic communities: a small but growing Hispanic community.

C. North City, MA
Population: 3,000,000
Schools: many good private schools. Public schools: average.
Employment: some industrial and service jobs; growth in technical and professional jobs.
Housing: apartments and flats, some single-family homes; average cost: $1,200/month.
Cultural events: many events of all kinds.
Ethnic communities: large communities of Hispanic, Asian, and European groups.

1. Look at the chart above, and answer the following questions:

a. Which city has more people, Marlo Park or Collegetown? ____________

How many more? ________________.

b. Which city has the most schools? __________ Are they better schools than in the other places?

c. Which city has the most employment opportunities for your friend than the others?

____

d. Which city is more expensive for housing than the other two? ________________

e. Which city offers more cultural events than the other two? ____________________

f. Which city has more ethnic diversity than the other two? _____________

2. What else do you need to know to make a decision about these cities?

____

____

3. *Which feature—employment, housing, cultural events, or ethnic communities—is most important? Why?*

____

____

4. *Rate the cities: Which is your favorite, next favorite, least favorite? Why?*

____

____

INTERACTIVITY 3 PREFERENCES ABOUT PLACES

1. *On the chart below, put a check mark in the column that shows your response to each statement:*

Statements	I strongly agree	It doesn't matter to me	I strongly disagree
a. I like to live in a large city.	______	______	______
b. I don't like small towns.	______	______	______
c. I want to find a high-paying job.	______	______	______
d. I want my children to go to good schools.	______	______	______
e. I feel comfortable with friends from my own ethnic community.	______	______	______
f. It's important to save money and not spend it on housing.	______	______	______
g. I like finding things to do near my home.	______	______	______
h. I'll go anywhere to find a good job.	______	______	______
i. I'll live anywhere to be with my family.	______	______	______
j. I'll stay where I am, even if I know a better place to live.	______	______	______

2. *Compare your chart with those of others in your group.*

3. *Explain to your group why you have chosen your own responses.*

4. *Try to reach an agreement about which statements and responses are most important. DO NOT EXPECT TO AGREE ABOUT EVERYTHING!*

INTERACTIVITY 4 GIVING REASONS FOR OPINIONS

1. With your group, choose the three most important statements in thinking about a place to live. Review your responses to the statements in InterActivity 3, and tell why you answered the way you did.

2. In the spaces below, report on your group's reactions to these three statements.

a. Our group agrees that these three statements are the most important:

____

____

____

b. Of these three, we agree on

____

____

____

c. We disagree on

____

____

____

After you have completed your sentences, show them to others in your group. When you receive your partner's sentences, read them carefully and ask him or her to explain any part that you do not understand. Then give the sentences back to your partner to make any needed changes.

3. Share your answers for step 2 with other members of the class.

INTER ACTIVITY 5 READ, WRITE, AND DISCUSS

Read the passage below as many times as you can in five minutes. After you have read the passage, cover it with a piece of paper, and write as much of it as you remember in the blank spaces below. Remember, you do not have to remember every word, but try to remember the meaning of the passage.

Charlie was a man who thought he was lucky in life. After all, he had a good job as an auto mechanic in a small garage. He lived in a two-bedroom apartment in North City with his wife, Elena, who worked as a receptionist, and two school-age children. He thought that in a few more years, with any luck, he could get a better job and make more money, maybe even start his own garage.

Then came trouble. The garage where he was working was sold to a large company. After a few months, the new company decided to sell the garage, and Charlie was out of a job. It was a hard time for the family. Charlie had to decide whether to look for another job in North City, or to move to a smaller town outside the city where there was a job that paid less money.

Charlie and Elena talked about the problem for many hours. Charlie didn't want to leave the city, because he thought that in a few years he would get a better job. Elena liked the idea of living in a town where the schools were better. Charlie liked being near his friends and places where he could meet his friends. Elena liked to think about the community swimming pool in the smaller town.

They are still talking about it.

1. Write the meaning in your own words.

____

____

____

____

____

____

____

2. What do you think they should do? Discuss your answer with your group.

INTER ACTIVITY 6 WRITING YOUR OPINION

It is not easy to make decisions, unless we have thought of all sides of the question. In this InterActivity, you are going to write your advice to Charlie and Elena about the choices described in InterActivity 5. Before you decide what to write,

1. Brainstorm about some of these questions.

a. Are job opportunities better in small towns or in cities? Will Elena have to find a new job?

b. Are the schools in small towns better than the ones in cities?

c. How important is it to be close to friends and family?

d. Will Charlie and Elena feel lonely if they move away from their own community in the city to a new community in the small town?

e. Will the family still find ways to fill their time in the new community?

*2. Draft: **When you have thought about the questions above, and any others that you think are important, write a draft of a letter to Charlie and Elena in the space below, in which you advise them what to do. Remember to include good reasons for your advice, and tell why the choice you advise is better than other possible choices.***

3. *Pair-edit:* *After you have completed a draft of your letter, exchange letters with a classmate. As you read your classmate's letter, see if you agree with his or her advice and reasons. If you do NOT agree, or if you do not understand what the letter says, write notes in the spaces between the lines. This time, do not mark grammar or spelling errors.*

4. *Rewrite:* *When you get your draft back from your classmate, you will probably want to revise your letter. Rewrite the letter, and make any changes necessary to make your letter clearer and easier to understand.*

5. *Proofread:* *When you have finished revising, exchange the letter with a different classmate. This time, read the classmate's letter carefully for grammar and spelling mistakes. If you find any, make the corrections in pencil on the paper, and give the paper back to the writer. It would be helpful to write encouraging comments at the bottom, or suggestions for specific changes to sentences, if you have any.*

6. *When you get your paper back the second time, make the necessary changes, and hand it in to the teacher.*

To the Teacher: You may want to help students get started by presenting a model of the start of a letter. For example:

(Today's Date)____________

Dear Elena and Charlie,

I have heard about your problem, and I have some suggestions that you might want to consider.

When students have completed their second drafts, you may want to share the letters, or the suggestions, with the whole class.

Unit 11 HOW CAN I DESCRIBE IT?

WHOLE CLASS

PRESENTATION LET'S TALK ABOUT DESCRIPTIONS

There are times when we have to describe things and people. In this Unit, we will find out how to use descriptions of objects, people, and places.

WHAT YOU NEED TO KNOW:

Words to describe articles of clothing

Size: small, medium, large

Shape: slim, bulky, men's or women's

Color: plain, patterned, striped, brown, beige, black, etc.

Material: cotton, wool, leather, nylon, etc.

Answer the following questions:

1. Look on the opposite page at the picture of a Lost and Found department in a large store. What do you think the man is looking for?

____

2. Fill in the chart below with words to describe items in the picture.

Item:	Size:	Shape:	Color:	Material:
a sweater	________	________	________	________
a handbag	________	________	________	________
a coat	________	________	________	________
an umbrella	________	________	________	________
a package	________	________	________	________

3. Now describe an item of clothing you are wearing or that you are carrying. Use words from the chart above, or other descriptive words. For example, you may describe a handbag as large, brown, leather, and with two long straps. Write your descriptions here:

____

INTER ACTIVITY 1 DESCRIBING "LOST" OBJECTS

WHAT YOU NEED TO BRING:

An item of clothing that you feel you can describe well.

Before class, give the item to your teacher. The teacher puts the items in one place at the front of the class.

With a group, imagine that you are at a department store Lost and Found counter. Fill in the chart below with words that describe your group's items.

	Item:	Size:	Color:	Material:	Shape:
	Raincoat	large	blue	cotton	men's
a.	________	________	________	________	________
		________	________	________	________
b.	________	________	________	________	________
		________	________	________	________
c.	________	________	________	________	________
		________	________	________	________
d.	________	________	________	________	________
		________	________	________	________
e.	________	________	________	________	________
		________	________	________	________

Choose one person in your group to play the role of the counter attendant. One counter attendant from each of two groups goes to the "counter" at the front of the class. The other students in each group take turns describing the objects which they "lost," using the words on the chart—for example, "I lost a large blue men's raincoat." The counter persons go "to the back" and try to find the correct items, one at a time. When a counter person has found an item, he or she holds it up and asks, "Is this the item that you lost?"

Other groups take notes and write down other ways to describe the items. After the first groups have "found" their items, the class discusses what happened, looks at their notes, and thinks about how to make the descriptions clearer. Then the other groups take their turn at the "Lost and Found."

INTER ACTIVITY 2 FINDING OUT WHAT IS FOR SALE

With your group, study the four examples of newspaper advertisements that you see on this page. Discuss what you think each ad means. Choose one item and describe it to the others in your group without looking at the page.

1. For each ad, write the information in the space provided. If you don't understand the abbreviations, ask your teacher.

Newspaper Advertisements

a.

needs tlc, will take first 2K dollars.

93 Chevy Camaro, red, 2-dr. conv., auto, stereo, pwr brakes, lo miles, 8K or b.o.

93 Chevy Caprice, runs and drives great, air, auto,

b.

ready to haul away. Asking $500 o.b.o.

Magi-cool refrigerator, 1990 model. 19" wide x 33" high, runs fine. Perfect for student's room. Selling as is, no delivery. $100

Gas range, Good shape. 4 burners, needs control

c.

excellent condition. Must see to appreciate.

Trutone stereo, almost new, radio, CD-player, cassette, w/ speakers. Will sell or trade for a small television. Asking $300 or best offer.

Stereo receiver, f.m. like

d.

Worn only twice. This is a real bargain. $1,200

Fur coat, women's alpaca, size 12. very warm, light weight, silk lining. Only one owner. Will sacrifice at $200 or best offer.

Fur coat, very old and in

Item:	Description:	Price:	Good buy?
a. ____________	____________	____________	____________
	____________	____________	____________
	____________	____________	____________
b. ____________	____________	____________	____________
	____________	____________	____________
	____________	____________	____________
c. ____________	____________	____________	____________
	____________	____________	____________
	____________	____________	____________
d. ____________	____________	____________	____________
	____________	____________	____________
	____________	____________	____________

2. What other information would you like to know about these items?

____

____

____

3. In a short paragraph, tell which item is the best buy and why you think so.

INTER ACTIVITY 3 WRITING ADS

With a partner, use a separate piece of paper to make drafts of advertisements for two items that you may want to sell—for example, a car, a bicycle, a stereo, or a piece of furniture. Remember that you must include important features like the color, how old the item is, and the price. Make your description as interesting as possible so that many people will respond to your ad.

After you finish your drafts, show them to other people in your group for their comments. When you have discussed how to improve your ads, rewrite them, making any necessary changes.

1. When the ads are ready, write them in the space below.

2. Compare your ads with your classmates' ads.

INTER ACTIVITY 4 DESCRIBING A PERSON

WHAT YOU NEED TO KNOW:

Words to Describe People

Hair Color: black, blond, brown, curly, wavy, straight
Size: short, small, medium height, tall, slim, large
Face: round, oval, freckled, dark, tanned, smooth, bearded

In a group, describe any of your classmates in no more than three sentences. Describe only the external appearance of the person, including hair color, clothes, possessions, and anything special about that person. Write out your description in the space below.

____

____

____

____

____

____

When everyone in the group has finished, read your description aloud to the group, and find out whether other people can identify the person you have described. As you listen to these descriptions, comment on their accuracy, and offer other ways to describe the person. You may want to rewrite your description here:

____

____

____

____

____

____

As a follow-up for homework, write a three-sentence description of yourself, and bring it back to your group at the next class.

INTER ACTIVITY 5 DESCRIBING PEOPLE YOU KNOW

In the space below, write a description of three people whom you like and know well, or whom you work with every day. Be sure to include their physical descriptions, their occupations, their personalities, and why you like them.

Read your paragraph aloud to your group. The other people will listen and ask questions to complete the descriptions. After you have responded to the group's questions, revise your paragraph, making any necessary changes.

Share your final description with other members of the class.

INTER ACTIVITY 6 DESCRIBING A FAVORITE PLACE

1. *With a partner, describe your favorite place. It may be a room, a restaurant, a theater, a part of a building, a place in a park, or any other place where you like to spend time.*

As you describe the place, your partner will be making a drawing of it. Your partner will ask you questions to complete the picture—for example, what furniture is in the room? What pictures or decorations are on the wall? What kind of lamps are in the room? If the place is outdoors, what kinds of trees and plants are there? What other features are in the place? (Use the space below for drawings.)

2. *After finishing your description, exchange roles, and listen and draw while your partner describes a favorite place. Exchange drawings and see if they are accurate.*

3. *When you have both finished your drawings and descriptions, share them with the others in the group. You tell about your PARTNER'S favorite place, pointing to the picture you have made. Then your partner tells about YOUR favorite place.*

4. *Write a paragraph in which you describe the place you like.*

INTER ACTIVITY 7 WRITING AN AD FOR A "DREAM VACATION"

WHAT YOU NEED TO BRING:

pictures of your favorite vacation spot	scissors and glue or paste	a large piece of poster paper	colored markers to make a poster
			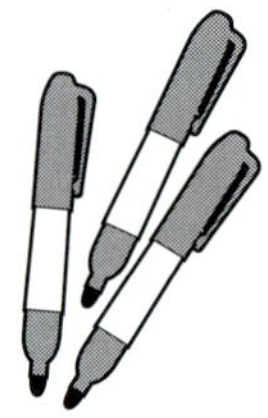

Form groups of people who have similar choices of favorite vacation spots.

1. *Brainstorm: In your group, tell about the important features that make you like the spot, like the location: the beaches, lakes, mountains, or other attractions; the sports facilities; the night life and restaurants; and any other special attractions. Describe the hotel rooms, including the beds, baths, views, and any other attractive features. Don't forget to mention the cost, including any special package deals for transportation.*

2. *Draft: Write a draft of your description in the space below, including the features your group has discussed, and compare it with your group's descriptions.*

3. *Pair-edit and rewrite:* *Read your description aloud to the other people in your group. Note any changes that you think are necessary to improve the draft. Then rewrite the draft on a separate piece of paper and give it to the teacher.*

4. *Find pictures to use as illustrations for your advertisement.* *You may want to use photographs you have taken yourself, or pictures taken from magazines or travel brochures. You may want to make drawings of your favorite place by yourself.*

5. *Finally, make a poster.* *Include both your final description and pictures, and any drawings you can create to make the poster attractive. Make a presentation of the poster to your classmates, and try to convince them to go on your vacation! The class will vote on the best presentation.*

Unit 12 WHAT'S YOUR ADVICE?

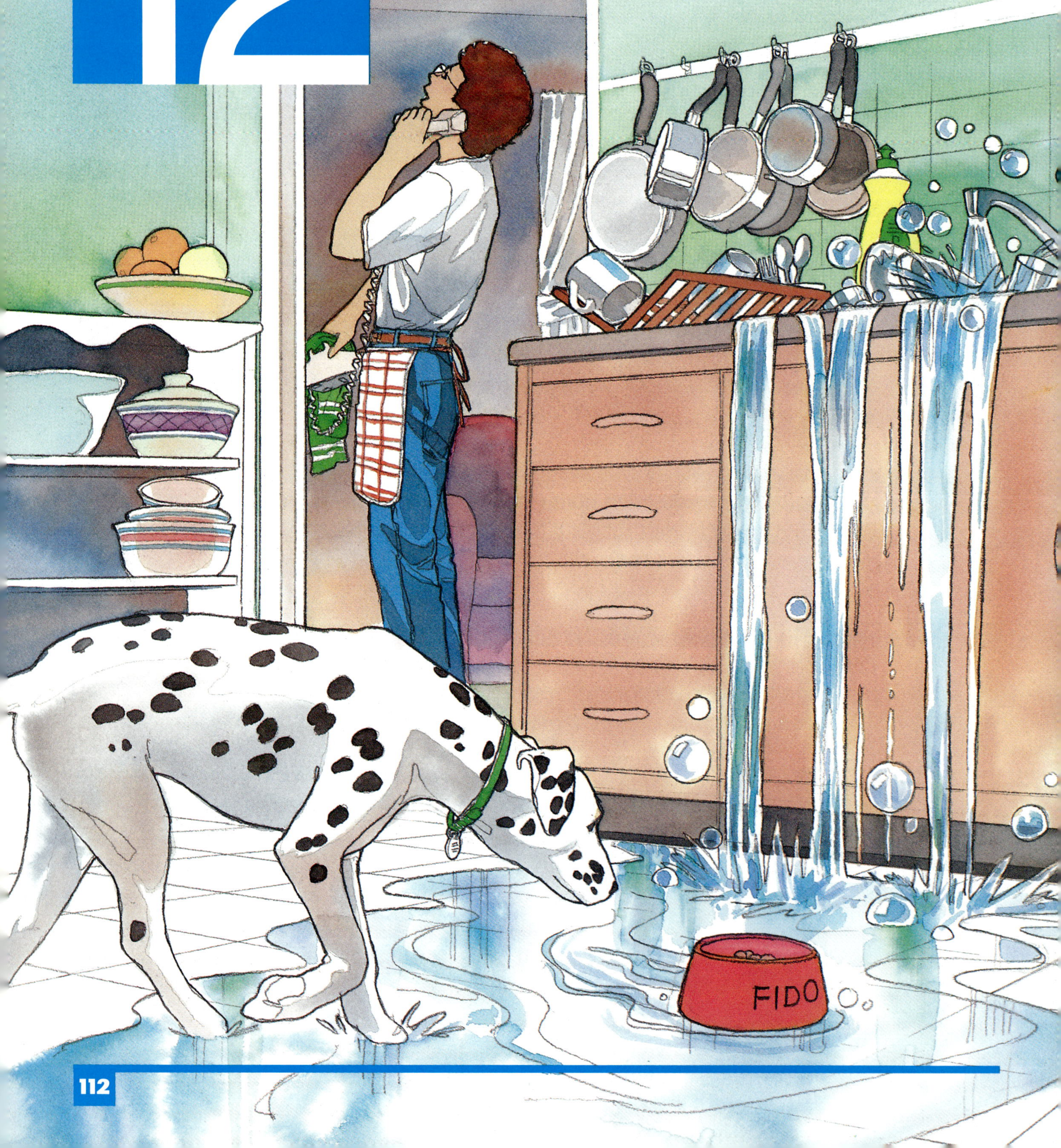

WHOLE CLASS

PRESENTATION LET'S TALK ABOUT INFERENCES

As we look at the picture on the opposite page, we can see that something has happened. Notice the dishes in the sink and the water overflowing onto the floor. Now notice the man in the next room talking on the telephone. He's holding a washrag in his hand, and he doesn't notice that the water is overflowing the sink.

Answer the following questions:

1. What do you think must have happened? Make an educated guess, and write it in the space below:

____

____

____

____

____

____

____

____

____

____

____

2. Now compare your guess with those of others in your class. Which explanations do you think are probably accurate? Which ones are probably not accurate? Write your favorite explanation below:

____

____

____

We call educated guesses and explanations like the ones above "inferences." In this Unit, we are going to learn about making inferences and talking about them.

INTER ACTIVITY 1 SHORT MYSTERIES

Below are some very short stories. The stories are mysteries because they don't explain what happened, but we can make inferences.

a. With a partner, read each story, and make inferences that explain the situation.

b. Write your inferences in the space below each story.

c. When you have finished, compare your inferences with those of your partner. Try to decide which inference makes a better explanation, and why.

d. Then explain your inference to your classmates.

1. Give your best solution to the following mysteries:

Mystery A.
I was a stranger in the town, and didn't know the local customs. I guess I should have known better, but I was still surprised to see all the businesses closed, and on a weekday in July. I looked around for someone to ask, but all I could find were some children dressed in red, white, and blue costumes, who said they were heading for a parade. What could it be?

____

____

____

____

Mystery B.
Why am I late? I am as regular as a clock: Every day I have breakfast at 7 a.m. and take the bus to work, just in time to arrive at 7:55, even before the boss gets there. But today, when it's a beautiful spring day, everyone's laughing at me, and all because I'm a full hour late. I'm so embarrassed! What could have happened?

____

____

____

____

Mystery C.
It was supposed to be such a nice day: they would take a nice stroll downtown, and look at the Christmas decorations that were just going up the day after Thanksgiving. But look at the crowds of people, all rushing to get to the stores. It's Friday—why aren't they at work, and what's all the fuss?

____

____

____

____

Mystery D.
When we returned home that night, after visiting my parents, we knew something was wrong right away. The door was open, the lights were turned on in the bedroom, and the stereo in the living room was missing. We thought that a thief had come in, but then we saw a note on the living room table that said, "Be right back." What could have happened?

____

____

____

____

Mystery E.
It was so frustrating! And after all the envious attention she had received from Susie. She looked everywhere for that scarf—under the bed, in the coat she wore last night, all around the house. She even called her friends who had hosted the party to ask if they found a scarf. But no luck, they didn't have it. Where could it be?

____

____

____

____

2. With your group, make up your own mystery, and try it on the other groups.

INTERACTIVITY 2 SAYINGS ABOUT INFERENCES

WHAT YOU NEED TO KNOW:

Saying: A well-known statement that tells an important truth.

1. Here is a list of sayings in English about inferences. With a small group, read each one, and explain what it means:

a. "Look before you leap."

b. "You can't tell a book by its cover."

c. "If it walks like a duck and talks like a duck, it must be a duck."

d. "Where there's smoke, there's fire."

e. "Don't jump to conclusions."

2. Many cultures have sayings about inferences. In the space below, write any other sayings you know on the subject of inferences:

____

____

____

____

Read your sayings to the others in your group, and explain their meaning. Do the sayings all agree about being careful when we make inferences?

3. Choose one of these sayings about inferences, and think of a story that shows its meaning. Tell your story to your group.

INTER ACTIVITY 3 ADVICE COLUMN

In many newspapers, there is a column of letters from readers where people ask advice for personal problems they are having.

1. With your group, discuss the three "Dear Andy" letters.

a. Read the first of the letters, and talk about it with your group. What is the problem? Make an inference that answers this question. Make sure that the members of the group agree on the answer, but be careful not to "jump to conclusions." Write the problem in the space labeled "Problem."
b. Write out your advice to the writer of the letter in the space labeled "Advice."
c. When you have written your advice, compare it with the advice that others in your group have written. Decide which advice is the best.
d. When you have finished the discussion of one letter, go on to the next.

Dear Andy: I am embarrassed about my English. Even though I study very hard, I still feel afraid to answer the telephone, because I don't think I can make people understand me. Sometimes when the telephone rings, I don't answer it because I am too afraid. Then people around me start to laugh at me. What can I do? —Afraid to Phone

Problem: ______________________________

Advice: ______________________________

____

Dear Andy: I am sixteen years old, and I know how to drive a car. I'd like to buy a car so that I can drive to work in a city nearby. If I can get the job, I can pay for the car, the fuel, and the insurance. But my parents say that I am too young for a car. If I had the job, I could give my parents some money to help pay the bills. What should I do? —Waiting for Wheels

Problem: ______________________________

Advice: ______________________________

____

Dear Andy: There is someone I see every day who bothers me. Every time I pass by his desk, he always says something that annoys me. But I cannot avoid him because his desk is between my desk and the door. When I ask my friends, they tell me to ignore him, but he just keeps annoying me. What should I do? —Fed Up

Problem: ______________________________

Advice: ______________________________

____

INTER ACTIVITY 4 SOLVING PROBLEMS

Here are some situations that many people face every day. You may recognize some of these problems, and you may have some good solutions.

1. In your group, discuss problems A-D.

a. With a partner, read through each problem, one at a time, and discuss possible reasons for the problem.
b. Tell what you think the people should do to solve the problem. Write your solutions in the spaces below.
c. When you have finished discussing all the problems, compare your solutions to those of other people in your group, and see if you can reach agreement.

A. "Maria is always late. No matter which day it is, she is always at least ten minutes late for work. The other people have to wait for her to arrive before they can start."

____

____

B. "Whenever I go to the store to buy something, I forget what I came for!"

____

____

C. "His work area is such a mess! Whenever I ask him for something, he has to spend five minutes looking for it."

____

____

D. "Her problem is that she never gets enough work done."

____

____

2. Think of a problem like the ones above. In your group, think of some possible reasons for the problem and some possible solutions.

INTER ACTIVITY 5 READ, WRITE, AND DISCUSS

Read the following passage as many times as you can in five minutes. After you have finished reading, cover the passage and write down what you can remember of it. Don't worry if you can't remember every word.

For a long time, none of us could figure out what was wrong, not even Sam, our big, furry cat, who loved Jack and always jumped on his lap. Every day Jack would come into the cafe, sit down to his cup of coffee, and start telling us the latest news. Jack was always good at telling stories, and told them in a way that would make us all laugh. But after five minutes he would start to sneeze, his eyes would water, and he would start scratching. We told him to do lots of things: stop drinking coffee, get more exercise, take aspirin. But nothing worked. For a while, Jack kept coming every day, but he kept getting worse. He blamed all of us for his troubles, even Sam.

Then one day Sam disappeared, probably after losing a fight. We were all very sad to lose such a great mouse hunter, so we were feeling low. Jack came into the cafe a few days later, to cheer us up. He told a few jokes, and we all started to feel better, even Jack. In fact, Jack wasn't sneezing or crying or scratching anymore.

"Jack, what happened? You're not sneezing," we said.

"Guess it was that darned cat," he said. "I guess I was allergic to Sam!"

1. Now write down the meaning of the passage in your own words:

___

___

___

___

___

___

___

___

___

2. When you have finished writing, compare your paragraph with those of other people in your group, and with the original passage.

INTER ACTIVITY 6 WRITING A LETTER OF ADVICE

Often we are called on to write a letter of advice to help solve a problem. Such letters are often difficult to write, because we don't know all the facts, and we don't always know what to tell the other person. Here are some problems that people often ask advice about:

"I'm always too busy. How can I find more time for my family, and for relaxation?"

"I wish I could get along better with my supervisor. She's always so demanding."

"I just don't understand teenagers. How can you talk to them?"

"My parents are getting older, but I don't know what to do to take care of them."

"How can my spouse and I both work and raise our young children properly?"

1. Brainstorm: *With a group, choose one of these problems. Make some inferences about the reasons for this problem. Be sure to note down what people say.*

Inferences:

a. ________________________________

b. ________________________________

c. ________________________________

d. ________________________________

2. Organize: *With a partner, think of some ways of solving the problem. Remember, your solutions will depend on the inferences you have made, so be careful not to jump to conclusions.*

Ways to solve the problem:

a. ________________________________

b. ________________________________

c. ________________________________

d. ________________________________

3. Draft: *Write a draft of your letter in the space below:*

4. Pair-edit: *Give your draft to your partner. Ask him or her to read your draft carefully, and to tell you about any mistakes. As you read your partner's letter, make sure it says what your partner means to say. Mark with a pencil any parts of the letter that you think need changes, and return the draft to the writer.*

5. Rewrite: *Write your draft over again on a separate piece of paper, this time including all the changes you made in the first draft.*

6. Proofread: *Before you submit the rewritten draft to the teacher, ask a partner to go over your paper with you carefully, to see if you have made any grammar or spelling errors. When you are satisfied with your draft, hand it in to the teacher.*

Unit 13 WHAT DO YOU DO IN YOUR SPARE TIME?

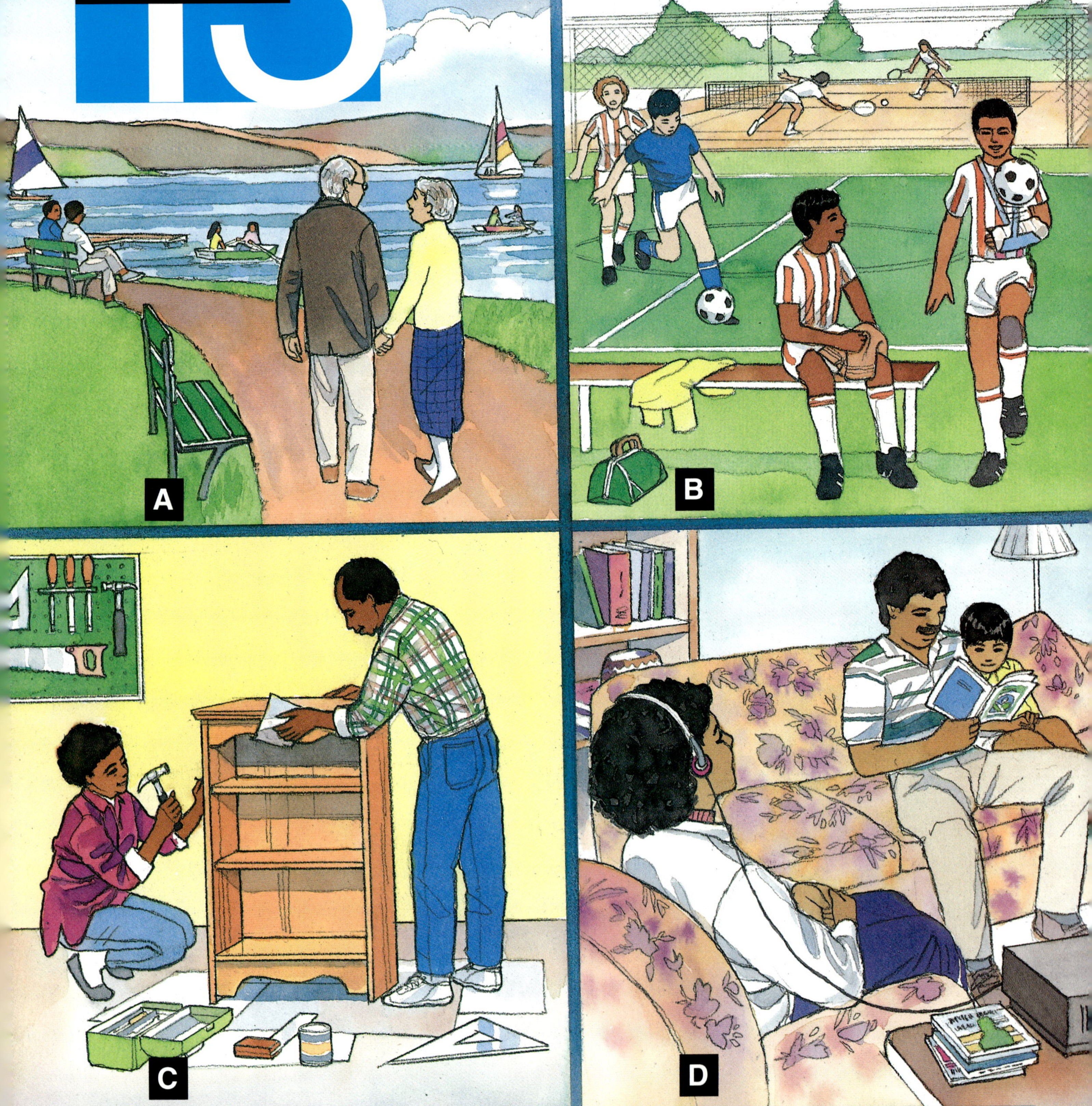

WHOLE CLASS PRESENTATION LET'S TALK ABOUT LEISURE ACTIVITIES

As modern machines make workers more efficient, we no longer have to work so many hours each week. This means that we have more time for our leisure. As time goes by, we will need to find more and more ways to spend our leisure time so that we may enjoy our lives.

1. Look at the pictures on the opposite page. Answer the following questions.

a. How are the people in Picture A enjoying their leisure time? ______________________

____

Where do you think they are? ______________________

What place does this remind you of? ______________________

What kinds of leisure activities can we enjoy there? ______________________

____

b. Now look at Picture B. How are the people enjoying their leisure time? ____________

____

Where do you think they are? ______________________

What place does this remind you of? ______________________

What kinds of leisure activities can we enjoy there? ______________________

____

2. Answer the same questions for Picture C and Picture D.

3. Write a list of your favorite ways of spending your leisure time. Compare your list with other classmates' lists.

____

____

____

____

INTER ACTIVITY 1 IDENTIFYING SIMILAR INTERESTS

Form a group made up of people in your class who enjoy a similar interest. If there are many people who enjoy the same activities, divide the group into smaller groups so that there are four or five people in each group.

With your group, discuss what you like about the leisure activity you share. In the space below, make a list of all the different reasons why you enjoy the activity. For example, if you like camping, you may have some of the following reasons:

a. I like to be outside in the fresh air.

b. I like to walk for exercise.

c. I like to be in a natural place, with lots of trees, plants, mountains, and streams.

d. Sometimes I like to get away from the crowds of people.

e. I like to spend time with my family or close friends.

Now list some of the reasons why your group likes this leisure activity:

INTERACTIVITY 2 GETTING READY FOR LEISURE ACTIVITIES

Some leisure activities are easy to prepare for, but others take more time. With your interest group from InterActivity 1, discuss what a person needs to do to prepare to enjoy the activity you have chosen. For example:

If you want to go camping, you will need to make a list of the things necessary for a happy trip, including a backpack, a sleeping bag, a tent, water, food, warm clothing, good walking shoes, and a flashlight.

When camping, remember to tell someone where you are going. Never camp alone, and always carry a first-aid kit with you.

1. *In the spaces below, list the things that are necessary to prepare for your activity so that you will have a good time:*

____

____

____

____

____

____

____

____

2. *What are some of the things you need be careful about in your favorite leisure activity?*

____

____

____

____

INTER ACTIVITY 3 MAKING A PRESENTATION ABOUT YOUR FAVORITE ACTIVITY

1. When your group has completed InterActivities 1 and 2, make a presentation about your activity to the rest of the class. Use the following list as a guide:

a. In your presentation, be sure to include a description of the reasons why you enjoy the activity, and the things you need to prepare for the activity.

b. You should also include some of the precautions we should take to avoid the dangers or drawbacks of this activity.

c. In giving your presentation, be sure that everyone in the group participates. Choose one member of the group to speak first and to introduce the first topic. When the first speaker finishes, he or she should introduce the next speaker, and so on to the last speaker. The last speaker should make a concluding statement that tells why this activity is your favorite.

d. You may improve your presentation by bringing pictures or objects to show the class more about the activity—for example, camping pictures.

2. In the space below, write an outline of how your presentation will be organized. Who will speak first? What will he or she say? Who will speak next? What will he or she say? And so on.

Speakers	Topics
1. ______________________	______________________
	______________________
2. ______________________	______________________
	______________________
3. ______________________	______________________
	______________________
4. ______________________	______________________
	______________________
5. ______________________	______________________
	______________________

INTERACTIVITY 4 INTERVIEWING OTHERS

Identify four "experts"—that is, class members who have knowledge or skill in a particular activity. For example, one person may know a lot about wood carving; another may be an expert in dancing. The "experts" will prepare to answer questions about their special activities. The teacher may serve as one of the "experts."

Form a new fact-finding group made up of people with different interests. This group will be different from your earlier group in InterActivities 1-3.

In your group, make a list of questions you want to ask about the new activities. You may want to find out about the equipment necessary, the time it takes to learn how to do the activity, whether there are places nearby to do the activity, how much it costs to participate, whether families with children can enjoy themselves, and so on.

1. Make a list of the questions you want to ask in the space below:

____

____

____

____

____

____

____

2. When your group has made a list of questions, teams will interview the class "experts," like this:

a. First divide your group into teams of two members, and send each team to a different "expert."

b. The team members will ask your group's questions to one of the "experts."

c. They will write the answers to the questions on a separate piece of paper.

d. When they finish, they will bring the answers back to the group.

INTERACTIVITY 5 EVALUATING RESULTS

After all the groups have completed InterActivity 4, each group will listen to the reports of the fact-finding teams about the new activities.

The teams will each tell what the answers were to the questions they wrote in InterActivity 4. After you listen to the teams' reports on each activity, discuss the activity and decide if you are interested in it. Why does that activity interest you, and what other questions do you have about it?

1. In the chart below, list the reasons why you are interested in the activities.

Activity	What's interesting about it?	What else would we like to know about it?

2. The fact-finding teams return to the "experts" to find answers to new questions from the group. Write these questions in the space below:

INTERACTIVITY 6 WRITING A SHORT REACTION PAPER

Choose an activity that you want to describe from those you studied in InterActivity 5. Write a short paragraph in which you tell why this activity interests you. In your reaction paragraph, give the reasons why you might like this activity, and also what else you want to find out about it.

1. Write your paragraph in the space below:

2. Share your paragraph with other people in your group. Find out if they are also interested in this activity.

INTERACTIVITY 7 WRITING AN EXPOSITORY PAPER

Write a paper in which you explain why you prefer one leisure activity over others. Use the following steps:

1. Brainstorm: ***In your group, tell about the important features that explain why you prefer one special leisure activity over the others you have found out about.***

a. Be sure to include the reasons you identified in InterActivity 1. Tell how to get started with this activity.

b. Include the steps needed to prepare for the activity and any equipment that is necessary, as you did in InterActivity 2.

c. Remember to include any needed precautions for people getting started, so they will enjoy the activity.

d. Make a concluding sentence in which you encourage people to get started in your activity. For example, you might write:

"I hope everyone can discover how much fun they can have with this activity."

2. Draft: ***Write a draft of your description in the space below, including the features your group has discussed:***

3. *Pair-edit, proofread, and rewrite:* ***Read your paper aloud to the other people in your group. Note any changes that you think are necessary to improve the draft. Then rewrite the draft on a separate piece of paper and give it to the teacher.***

To the Teacher: You might want to meet with students to discuss their writing. In your meeting, you may want to ask each student these questions:

a. "What are your strengths as a writer? What things do you do best?"

b "How well have you organized your writing to say the things you want to say?"

c. "How can you improve your organization to make your writing clearer to the reader?"

d. "Which are the most serious sentence-level mistakes in your writing?" There may be some special problems the student can work on.

e. "What special techniques might you use to help improve your writing? Should you write more letters to people? Should you reread your paper several times before you rewrite it? Should you rewrite your papers more times? Should you show your writing to other people before you rewrite?"

You may also have some special advice for the student.

Unit 14

WHAT WILL TOMORROW BE LIKE?

WHOLE CLASS

PRESENTATION FUTURE CLASSROOMS

The classroom of the future is probably going to look much different from the one you are in today. The teacher may be on a large television screen, or working with you at your desk computer. Books will be on small compact disks instead of paper. You will probably be able to answer questions over your telephone/computer, even if the teacher is in a studio very far away.

Answer the following questions:

1. Look at the picture on the opposite page, and compare the features of the "classroom of the future" with the classroom you are in now.

What are the advantages that you can see? ____________________

____

____

What are some of the disadvantages? ____________________

____

____

2. Will it be easier to learn to write when you have a computer to help you, or will it be more difficult?

____

Why do you think so? ____________________

____

3. Is it easier to learn if you are in a large classroom with many students, or if you are studying with a small group of people along with computers to help you?

____

____

4. What features would you like to see in the classroom of the future?

____

____

INTER ACTIVITY 1 HOW MACHINES CHANGE OUR LIVES

1. *With a group, discuss how life has changed because of the machines we now have in our homes. Look at the chart below, and write down what changes have come about because of the machines listed there.*

Machine	Before, we had to . . .	Now, we can . . .
typewriter	write only with a pen	write much faster
electronic calculator	______________	______________
	______________	______________
microwave oven	______________	______________
	______________	______________
food processor	______________	______________
	______________	______________
portable tape player	______________	______________
	______________	______________
automatic teller machine	______________	______________
	______________	______________
videocassette recorder (VCR)	______________	______________
______________	______________	______________
	______________	______________
______________	______________	______________
	______________	______________

2. *Add your own choices for machines in the blank spaces above. When you have completed the chart, write a short paragraph in the space below in which you describe the advantages of using the machines we have become familiar with in the last few years. (Use another piece of paper if necessary.)*

____

____

____

____

INTER ACTIVITY 2 A DAY'S WORK IN THE YEAR 2020

1. With a small group, discuss how work activity will change by the year 2020. In the chart below, answer the following questions about jobs today, compared with the jobs of the future:

Tasks	Who does it now?	In 2020?
answering telephones	receptionist	automated answering machine
typing letters	____________	____________
	____________	____________
delivering packages	____________	____________
	____________	____________
making clothes	____________	____________
	____________	____________
repairing machines	____________	____________
	____________	____________
teaching	____________	____________
	____________	____________
other tasks:	____________	____________
____________	____________	____________
	____________	____________

2. When you have completed the chart, write a paragraph on how you think jobs will change by the year 2020. Be sure to tell how new machines will help make the job easier. Also tell how the work you do will change in the future when new machines become available. (Use another piece of paper if you need more space.)

____

____

____

____

____

3. Now compare your paragraph with those of others in your group. Do you all see the same changes in the future?

INTER ACTIVITY 3 WHAT WILL HAPPEN TO FAMILY LIFE?

1. With a group, discuss how the changes of the past few years have affected family life.

Think of changes happening now to family life. How do you think these changes will affect families in the future?

2. Make your concerns into short statements about family life. For example,

Families won't gather together for dinner every night.
We won't live in the same home with grandparents.

With a partner, you are going to use the opinions chart below to help you find out what other people's attitudes are about these changes. Fill in the blank spaces under Statements with your own statements.

Statements	Better for families	No difference	Worse for families
In the future, families will watch more TV.	______	______	______
More women will work outside the home.	______	______	______
There will be more video games for children and adults.	______	______	______
Schools will be open all year long.	______	______	______
People will have more leisure time.	______	______	______
Your statements:			
______________________	______	______	______
______________________	______	______	______
______________________	______	______	______

3. When you and your partner have developed an opinions chart, interview the other members of your class, and record their responses.

4. After the interviews, discuss the results with your group.

INTERACTIVITY 4 REPORTING ON THE INTERVIEW

1. With one or two partners from your previous group, write a paragraph in the spaces below on what you found in your interview in InterActivity 3.

a. Tell how the people whom you interviewed answered the questions.

b. Be sure to include the comments they made.

c. Analyze the results by explaining why you think people answered the way they did.

2. Now compare your paragraph to those of others in your class.

Did other people find the same results as you and your partner(s) found?

INTER ACTIVITY 5 READ, WRITE, AND DISCUSS

Read the following passage as many times as you can in five minutes. After you have finished reading, cover the passage and write down what you can remember of it. Don't worry if you can't remember every word.

Several years ago, in a popular book called *Future Shock*, writer Alvin Toffler told us that the pace at which things are changing in our modern world causes trouble for many people. Today it takes hours to travel to places that used to take weeks or months to get to. We can listen, talk, and even see people on different continents at the same time. We can send copies of pictures electronically to each other over the telephone in seconds using a fax machine, compared to the days it took to send pictures just a few years ago.

There are many advantages to living in the age of rapid technological improvements. Inventions like the microwave oven and the food processor have made food preparation easier. The bar-code readers in supermarkets have made lines at check-out counters move faster, and given us clear records of what we buy. Compact disk recordings have given us better vision and sound for our televisions and stereos. New industries, like the computer manufacturing industry, have grown rapidly in the last few years, replacing older factories and making hard jobs easier.

But there are disadvantages to "future shock." Some of the jobs that people used to have are now done by machine. In the automobile industry, automatic machines have replaced human workers in many places on the production line, because the machines are more efficient. Computers can do in seconds the work that office workers used to do, so there is no longer a need for the same kinds of jobs in offices. In many countries, there are more unemployed people, because the kinds of jobs they used to have are no longer needed.

In order to prepare for the future, we have to retrain ourselves now for tomorrow's technology. We must learn how to use the new machines, and make them work for us. Today's children will soon become the workers of the future. They need to have our guidance to make the future a place where technology serves us all, not where it takes away our power. We must learn how to overcome future shock.

1. Write down the meaning of the passage in your own words:

____

____

____

____

____

____

2. When you have finished writing, compare your paragraph with your partner's paragraph. See whether you have remembered the same parts of the reading passage.

INTER ACTIVITY 6 PROBLEMS OF THE FUTURE

1. With a partner, think about coping with future changes in transportation, jobs, and education. Write out your answers in the spaces provided.

What would happen if

a. your employer asked you to use a computer on the job?

b. there were more labor-saving machines where you work?

2. Now make up some questions of your own. Write them in the space below:

3. Now ask the other members of the group your questions. How did people respond to your questions? What were some of the answers?

INTER ACTIVITY 7 WHAT WILL THE FUTURE BRING?

With a group, discuss how new products will affect life in the year 2020. You may want to concentrate on the workplace, the home, or the classroom.

1. *Brainstorm:* *Think about how new machines have already changed our present lives. How will newer machines affect our lives in the future? Discuss the advantages as well as the disadvantages of such machines. For example, machines make work more efficient, but they might cause people to lose their jobs.*

Describe the three most important changes that new machines will make, and explain how we should we deal with them:

2. *Draft.* *Write a draft of your description in the space below, including the ideas that your group discussed in the brainstorming step:*

3. Pair-edit, proofread, and rewrite: ***Read your paper aloud to the other people in your group. Note any changes that you think are necessary to improve the draft. Then rewrite the draft on a separate piece of paper and give it to the teacher.***

To the Teacher: You may wish to meet with the student to discuss his or her writing. In your meeting, you may want to ask these questions:

a. "How well have you organized your writing to say the things you want to say?"

b. "How can you improve your organization to make your writing clearer to the reader?"

c. "Which are the most serious sentence-level mistakes that are still in your writing?"

You may want to suggest additional special techniques to help the student improve his or her writing.

Unit 15 WHAT WORK IS IN YOUR FUTURE?

Now.

Five years from now.

WHOLE CLASS

PRESENTATION LET'S TALK ABOUT CHANGES

These days the future seems closer and closer to us. Changes in technology, in world events, and in the workplace are happening so fast that we must always look forward to the future.

Answer the following questions:

1. Look at the pictures on the opposite page. Identify the things you see in the picture labeled "Now":

____

Describe the person you see in the picture:

____

2. Now look at the picture labeled "Five years from now." Identify the things that are different from the first picture:

____

____

Some of the things in this picture are already familiar. How many of these "future" items do you recognize?

____

3. The person in both pictures is making a newsletter for her community group. How does she do that today?

____

____

According to the picture, how will she be able to do that in the future?

____

____

4. After she finishes designing the newsletter, she will send it out to the people in her community. How does she do that today?

____

____

How will she be able to do that in the future?

____

INTER ACTIVITY 1 PICTURING YOUR FUTURE WORKPLACE

1. With a group, think about the work you want to do five years from today. Then answer the following questions:

a. What kind of work will you be doing? ____________________

b. What will your workplace look like? What machines will you use? ____________________

____

c. Will you be working with other people? What will they be doing? ____________________

____

d. Will you be the supervisor, or will you be working with the others? ____________________

e. Will you have an office? What items will be in the office? ____________________

____

2. After your discussion, draw a picture in the space below of the workplace you have described above. Remember to include all of the items you have listed, as well as all of the people you have mentioned.

3. Now share your picture with the others in your group. Ask for their questions and comments.

INTERACTIVITY 2 PREPARING FOR THE FUTURE

1. With a partner, compare the pictures that each of you drew in InterActivity 1. Answer the following questions:

a. What things are similar about the two pictures? For example, do both pictures show offices? How many people are in each picture? What kinds of items and machines are in both pictures?

____

____

____

b. How do the two pictures differ? ______________________________

____

____

2. How would you describe the work that each person is doing in each picture? What activities is YOUR work going to include?

____

____

3. With your partner, write down a list of the things you will need to do to prepare for the work you have just described. Here are some terms that might help you make the list:

college courses	on-the-job training	home study	computer training
internship program	placement service	résumé	promotion

____

____

____

INTERACTIVITY 3 PUTTING STEPS TO A CAREER IN ORDER

1. In the future, people will be moving into new jobs. Here is a list of steps they must take to prepare for these jobs. With your partner, study the list of steps to a career in the chart below.

Steps to a Future Career

a. Prepare a résumé, a description of your work history.

b. Go to a job interview.

c. Find a good school to learn the skills you will need.

d. Decide which work situation is the best one for you.

e. Ask for a promotion.

f. Visit different work situations and talk to the people who work there.

g. Work as a trainee or intern in a work situation.

h. Apply for a position.

Discuss the steps, and arrange them in the best order. Write the letter of your first step next to 1 below, then write the letter of your second step next to 2, and so on.

Best order: 1. _____ 2. _____ 3. _____ 4. _____ 5. _____ 6. _____ 7. _____ 8. _____

2. Now write a list of career steps to prepare for the work that you described for yourself in InterActivity 2:

____

____

____

____

____

____

____

3. When you have finished your list of career steps, share it with your partner and ask for comments. You may want to make some changes.

INTER ACTIVITY 4 MAKING A FLOWCHART

Sometimes our plans include so many activities that we don't know what to do first. We can show the order of activities in a picture called a flowchart. For example, here is a flowchart of the process of writing papers that we have used in this book:

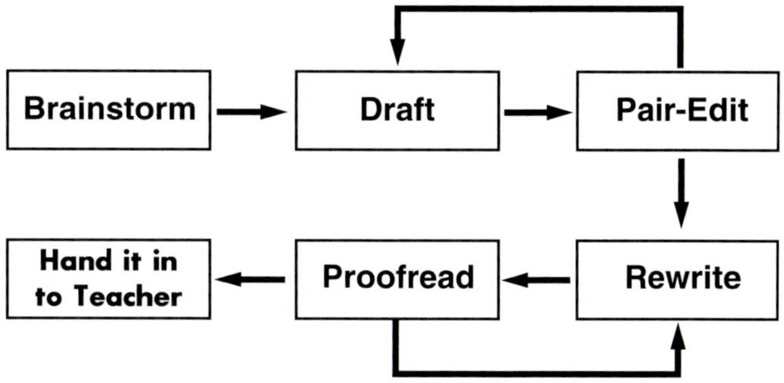

Notice that steps are sometimes repeated, and sometimes there are alternative choices in the sequence. These choices are shown by arrows in the chart.

1. With a group, discuss the following process for planning a picnic:

a. You meet your friends and decide to have a picnic.

b. You make a list of all the food, drinks, and equipment (blankets, coolers, umbrellas, etc.) you will need for the picnic.

c. You tell people to bring certain foods, drinks, and equipment.

d. You buy the food that you have agreed to bring.

e. You prepare the food or equipment that you agreed to bring, OR

f. You change your mind, and repeat c.

g. You go to the park for a picnic and have a great picnic, OR

h. If the weather is bad, you go somewhere indoors, OR

i. You repeat the whole process, starting with a.

2. Now design a flowchart in the space below to show the process. Remember to include the choices and the repeated steps.

3. When you have finished, share your chart with the others in your group.

INTER ACTIVITY 5 READ, WRITE, AND DISCUSS

Read the following passage as many times as you can in five minutes. When you finish reading, cover the paragraphs, and write down the meaning in your own words. Don't worry if you can't remember every word. Be sure to use complete sentences.

When the boss told Aki that he was going to close down the small factory where they had been working together for the past five years, Aki thought there would be trouble.

"What will I do now? Where will I find another job? The only job I ever had was in that factory. Now that it's gone, I don't know what to do."

For a few days, Aki did nothing. There were some jobs listed in the classified advertisements in the newspaper, but they didn't pay much money, and Aki could see that those jobs would soon end, just as the first one had ended.

But on the fourth day, Aki spotted an advertisement for a new career, computer-assisted design, CAD. By studying CAD, Aki could start designing tools and machines, and one day open a small factory!

And that's just what happened. Aki studied CAD, did an internship with a design company, sent out résumés, interviewed, and got a new job. After five years, it was time to open a small factory—Aki's Machines.

1. *Now cover the passage, and write down the meaning of the passage in your own words:*

2. *When you have finished writing, compare your paragraph with those of other people in your group, and with the original passage.*

INTERACTIVITY 6 CHOOSING WORK YOU LIKE

In this InterActivity, you are going to discover your preferences for working in the future. If you are looking for a new job, these preferences may help you decide which to choose.

1. Look at the careers in the chart below. For each career, put a check (√) in the column that shows how much you are interested in that career.

CAREERS:	I AM VERY INTERESTED	I AM INTERESTED	I'M NOT INTERESTED
accountant	______	______	______
administrative assistant	______	______	______
assembler	______	______	______
baker	______	______	______
bank teller	______	______	______
computer programmer	______	______	______
dental assistant	______	______	______
insurance agent	______	______	______
paralegal	______	______	______
machinist	______	______	______
office manager	______	______	______
medical technician	______	______	______
nurse	______	______	______
physical therapist	______	______	______
professional (doctor, lawyer, teacher, etc.)	______	______	______
salesperson	______	______	______
technician (repairs machines)	______	______	______

Think of other careers that you might be interested in.

2. With a small group, compare your responses to the chart above. For those items which you marked either "very interested" or "interested," answer the following questions:

a. How much training is necessary for this work? ______________________________

____

b. Where is this training offered? (In colleges only? On the job? In private training schools?)

(See next page.)

____

(InterActivity 6, continued.)

c. How much time and money does it require to get this training? ______________________

____

d. What are the rewards for doing this kind of work? (Good salary? Job security? Working with people? Working near to home? Chance for promotion?)

____

e. After I have the job, what problems might I find? ______________________________

____

3. After discussing your preferences with the group, you may want to change some of the preferences you listed on the chart. If so, repeat step 2 so you can find out about a different job category.

4. Ask other people in your class how to find more information about the jobs you have chosen.

INTER ACTIVITY 7 PLANS FOR THE FUTURE

In this InterActivity, you are going to report to your teacher on your career plan for the future. You may not actually follow this plan, but writing it will help you make future decisions about your work.

1. *Brainstorm:* ***Form a small group of people who have some of the same plans that you have for work in the future. For example, some people may be interested in professions, others in working in offices, some in factories or shops, or in other work. In your group, tell about your own plans for future work. Take turns answering the following questions:***

a. What kind of work do you like to do?

b. What are the rewards for this kind of work?

c. What job security does this work offer?

d. How will your family accept the work that you have chosen?

e. What steps will you need to take to prepare yourself for this work?

2. Draft: *In the space below, write a draft of a report to your teacher on the work you have chosen for the future. (If necessary, use extra paper.) In your draft, be sure to respond to the questions listed in Brainstorm:*

3. Pair-edit: *With a partner from your group, exchange drafts. Read your partner's draft carefully. Make sure that you understand everything in the draft, and that the writer has responded to all the questions clearly. If there are some parts that you do not understand, or that you think need to be made clearer, draw a circle around those parts.*

4. Rewrite and proofread: *When you have made the changes that your partner has suggested on your paper, rewrite the report on a separate piece of paper to hand in to the teacher. Before you hand it in, proofread the paper very carefully for small mistakes in grammar and spelling. Look carefully at the ends of words to make sure they are correct.*

5. When everything is correct, hand the paper in to the teacher.

To the Teacher: You may want ask the students to share their papers with the whole class, either by making copies, reading the papers aloud, or projecting them on an overhead projector.